DIAMOND GIRL:

A GUIDE TO BEGINNER AND ADVANCED SOFTBALL PITCHING

Donna Reiss

Copyright © 2011 Donna Reiss
All rights reserved, including the right to reproduce this book or any portions thereof.

Printed in the United States of America

ISBN: 1466234156
ISBN-13: 978-1466234154

DIAMOND GIRL:
A GUIDE TO BEGINNER AND ADVANCED SOFTBALL PITCHING

by Donna Reiss

CONTENTS

Preface	vii
Acknowledgements	ix
Introduction	xi

PART 1 – BEGINNER PITCHING

1	Strike Three – You're Out!	1
2	Proper Mechanics	3
3	Wrist Snap and Release	9
4	The Arm Circle	23
5	The Hip Turn	29
6	Balance	35
7	Stride	41
8	Pitching from the Pitching Rubber	45
9	Location! Location! Location!	47
10	Relaxation and Speed	51
11	Tips and Tricks for Beginners	55
12	Let's Have Some Fun!	59

PART II – ADVANCED PITCHING

13	Advanced Pitching: Adding Movement Pitches	63
	a) Review of the Fastball	64
	b) The Change-Up	66
	c) The Drop Pitch	71
	1. Slip or Peel Drop	72
	2. Turnover Drop	74
	d) The Rise Ball	75
	e) The Curve Ball	81
	f) The Screwball	84
14	The Pitcher/Catcher Team	87
15	Managing the Game	93
16	Going Back to Basics	99

Bibliography	101

PREFACE

"I'm too tired." "I don't feel like it." "It's too hot." "It's boring." Coaches and parents have heard all these excuses at one time or another from their daughters and/or players trying to get out of pitching practice. Unfortunately, in order to move from being classified as a "thrower" to a "pitcher," practice is a vital part not only for the athlete but for coaches and parents as well. That doesn't mean practices have to be boring. They need to be FUN! The learning process of pitching and developing practice regimens begins at a young age.

I came from a softball/baseball family – my uncle pitched in the Phillies minor league before World War II, my dad was a catcher in baseball and pitched fast-pitch softball, my brother pitched baseball and played fast-pitch softball, and my mom played fast-pitch softball in school. I never got to see most of them play as I was either "non-existent" or too small to remember. One thing I do remember is watching my brother pitch. While most 8-year old children were off playing on the playground at the ball fields, I was sitting behind home plate, watching my brother take charge of the game and the batters. I was amazed at the movement he could put on the ball, curving it in or out, making it drop or rise, as well as changing the velocity and location of each pitch. He forced the batters to go after pitches HE wanted them to attempt to hit. I loved watching batters trying to hit his "high heat," only to hear the popping sound of the ball hitting the catcher's mitt as they struck out.

Yes, at that age I was watching baseball, not softball. But, most importantly, I was *studying* how a pitcher keeps batters off the base path. Whether it is baseball or softball, the main objective of pitchers is the same.

When I reached high school, I made the junior varsity softball team as an outfielder. Between my freshman and sophomore year I had the crazy notion of trying to pitch. I watched the techniques of the pitchers on the varsity squad. I also watched my dad pitch and how he also worked the batters. My dad never pushed me into pitching. He seemed to sit back and watch, almost knowing that at some point I would also try it. My mother, on the other hand, had the typical motherly concern that I was going to get hurt.

That day finally came. I asked my dad to catch for me because I wanted to see if I could pitch. I threw the ball to his glove more times than not. My first thought was I can do this! That summer I practiced hard. It didn't make any difference if I had a catcher or not. I tried hitting a hole in our barn door. I pitched stones into a creek behind our house, trying to see how far down the creek I could throw them. I threw at our backyard tree, seeing if I could hit just the right spot to make the ball bounce right back to me. *I made practice fun!* I didn't have all the gizmos and gadgets pitchers use nowadays to improve their technique. The one thing I did have though was passion – the passion for the love of the game, and the passion to never stop improving.

Diamond Girl

Pitching was in my blood. The sights and sounds of a softball field, the smell of my glove, putting on my cleats, being handed the game ball – all got my adrenaline pumping. Looking back to those early years made me realize that my pitching success began because of fun! Those words - "I'm too tired," "I don't feel like it," "It's too hot," "It's boring," - never entered my mind.

Diamond Girl: A Guide to Beginner and Advanced Softball Pitching is broken into two parts – Part 1 for beginner pitchers, and Part 2 for advanced pitchers. The focus of the book is written with the intent of not only developing beginner and advanced pitchers but to show how you can make practice fun, with or without a catcher, with or without the use of a softball.

This book is for all ages, for all levels, as well as for coaches and parents. Chapters 1 through 8 review the basic mechanics of the wrist snap, the arm circle, the hip turn, and balance, building towards the actual pitching motion from the pitching mound. Chapters 9 and 10 review the importance of accuracy, ways to improve the location of your pitches, as well as relaxation of your arm to add velocity. Chapter 11 contains tips on ways to continue learning about pitching as well as common problems all pitchers face at times. Chapter 12 will show how to put fun into practicing and will probably be one of the most used chapters in this book. This chapter includes drills which use "teaching aids" such as potato chips, hockey pucks, and swimming pool rings.

Chapter 13 begins Part II - Advanced Pitching. Students learn about the necessity of adding moving pitches as well as drills for each pitch. Chapters 14 and 15 teach the importance of the pitcher/catcher team and the mental aspect of the game. Chapter 16 discusses ways to correct common pitching problems by going back to basics and indicates the drills that will correct specific problems.

"Ignite a spark and it will turn into a flame." As a coach, you need to ignite a spark in your *throwers* by getting them excited about pitching. The best reward for a coach is to watch those sparks grow into flames – your *pitchers*. It's amazing! This book does just that.

ACKNOWLEDGEMENTS

I would like to sincerely thank my husband, Curt, and my son, Justin, for their support and encouragement to write this book. Thank you also for being substitute catchers for some of my students when needed. Justin, your assistance with pitching clinics has been invaluable!

I sincerely thank my brother, Kenneth ("Lee") Gross, for being an inspiration and a role model. His practice and game ethics and baseball/softball knowledge in general, taught me important lessons in being a player and coach.

Thank you to Paul Hetrick and the Richland Area Softball Association (RASA) for giving me the opportunity and facilities to provide pitching lessons. Thanks to all my former and current students and their parents for their dedication and commitment to softball.

Thanks to my former teammates – the "old timers" from the original Allentown Patriot Lazers. We had such great times and learned a great deal from each other. I wouldn't have had the success as a pitcher without my catcher, Bernice ("Bingo") Bott.

I extend a very special thank you to Jaime Wolhbach for her insightful interview on pitching from a professional catcher's perspective.

Thank you, Samantha Laub, for being my model in the photos. Great job!

Finally, I can't say enough about the exceptional photography done by Judy Feher. Thank you so much!

INTRODUCTION

"No matter how good you think you are, there is always someone better," one of my early coaches told me. I've used this motto as a player and as a pitching coach, driving me to become a "student" of fast pitch pitching. I always wanted to be the best. I always wanted to be in control of the batters. As soon as I stepped across the base line at the beginning of the game, it was *my* game and the opposing team would need to take it away from me if they were going to win.

You see, a pitcher is only as good as she wants to be and that desire has to come from her heart. I possessed that passion and I try to impress upon my students this same quality. I do that by continuing to study new ways to motivate my students, sharing not only personal experiences but also knowledge gained over 26 years of pitching at various levels. I also learned from listening to speakers, such as Olympic pitchers and famous college coaches, at numerous national softball coaches' clinics. My coaching experiences at the high school and collegiate levels have proven to be invaluable as well.

The focus of this drill book is on fundamentals, improving your basic knowledge of skills needed to be a successful pitcher while having fun. It includes drills that I have learned from other instructors as well as a few of my own designed creations.

In order to make practicing a little more fun, at times we will use different "props," or teaching tools which may help to expedite the learning process. Instructions given in this book are for right-handed pitchers, but left-handers will find them easy to use with just minor adjustments.

CHAPTER 1:
Strike Three – You're Out!

You hear the umpire yell an emphatic "three!" as he punches the air with his fist. You watch the batter walk back to her dugout, feeling a sigh of relief as you realize you just struck out one of the toughest hitters in your league. The umpire's response sounds great to a young softball pitcher. That kind of success is an everyday occurrence to softball superstar pitchers like Jennie Finch and Cat Osterman.

Jennie Finch was a 3-time All American at the University of Arizona. She won 109 games posting a 32-0 record during her junior year and holds the NCAA record of 60 victories in a row during which she struck out 1,028 batters. She has been a member of the Team USA national team since 2002, and competed in the 2004 and 2008 Olympic games. Her ten-year career record in international competition is 36-2 with 397 strikeouts in 239.1 innings.

Catherine ("Cat") Osterman pitched a perfect game for her high school, striking out 21 batters in a row at age 17. After high school, she pitched for the University of Texas at Austin where she recorded 2,134 strikeouts during her four-year career. She pitched 20 NCAA career no-hitters and 10 NCAA career perfect games. (A no-hit game is one where the pitcher relinquishes no hits but allows a runner to get on base by a walk or hitting a batter. A perfect game is where the pitcher allows no batters to reach base for any reason.) She holds the NCAA record ERA of 0.5065. Cat participated in the 2004 Olympic Games in Athens, picking up two wins and a save for the U.S. gold medal team.

Were Jennie Finch and Cat Osterman natural athletes? Maybe. But just having natural abilities didn't make them pitchers. You see, there are actually two types of girls who step onto the pitching rubber. One type is a "thrower," a person who is satisfied to go out and just throw the ball and not put time into

Diamond Girl

practicing. The other is a "pitcher," a person who practices hard, enjoys what she's doing and wants to be the best she can be for her team and for herself. Jennie Finch and Cat Osterman are pitchers.

A pitcher will spend years in developing not only her physical skills but also the mental skills of the game - possessing the desire to be the best, wanting to continually improve, and playing the game with a passion. Both Jennie, who started pitching at age 8, and Cat, who began pitching at age 11, took the time to **develop** their talents and their athletic abilities to become pitchers. They started at an early age learning and practicing all the basic drills needed to become the stars of today.

No matter what age you are, if you are serious about softball pitching be patient and work hard to develop those skills. Pitching can be a very rewarding experience if you invest the time and hard work. Becoming a better pitcher begins with proper mechanics.

The instructions in this book are given for a right-handed pitcher. A left-handed pitcher can easily adapt by thinking the opposite of the directions, remembering that your stride foot (or knee, if you are in a kneeling position for a particular drill) and glove hand will always be positioned down the power line towards your catcher.

CHAPTER 2
Proper Mechanics

A team can be beat mentally before a game even begins just by seeing a specific pitcher walk onto the mound. This pitcher is poised and confident and is known to take control of the game through her control of the strike zone.

How did she earn that reputation? The common ground for success as a pitcher at any level - beginner, high school, college, or professional - is acquiring proper mechanics. Patience and practice are key since sound mechanics don't happen overnight. You need to *train* your muscles to remember where to release the ball, when to use hip rotation, and what stride length to use. This is called "muscle memory" and it is only achieved from many repetitions through practice. Muscle memory will also help prevent injuries to your pitching arm which is vital if you intend on a career as a pitcher.

Always remember to stretch before beginning any exercise or sports program, including not only your large muscles such as your legs, but also your arms, shoulders, back, and even your wrists. This will definitely help to reduce the possibility of injuries. Talking to your gym teacher or a trainer at a gym about creating an exercise program specifically for softball pitchers is also very helpful.

How often should you practice? Beginner pitchers should practice at least three times a week for 15 minutes, anywhere from 50 to 100 pitches. Of course, you won't practice every wrist snap drill in this book at one time. Once you feel comfortable with the first few drills, start adding new ones. As you mature as a pitcher, the duration of your practice sessions as well as frequency and pitch count (@ 100-200 pitches) will also increase.

Keep in mind that *quality* is better than *quantity*. Proper training of your muscles requires proper form (quality), not how quickly (quantity) you can go through each drill.

Diamond Girl

Can you still practice even if you don't have a catcher? Definitely YES! You can use a wall, a net, a tree, a barn door, even a tire hanging from a tree where you throw the ball through the hole! You can get your mom to hang an old sheet over a clothesline, anchoring the corners, and throwing at an "X" marked on the sheet. You can even roll tube socks into a ball and actually throw them at a mirror. This gives you the opportunity to watch your form. Dedicated pitchers are very resourceful in finding ways to practice. Be creative!

Basic Fundamentals of the Pitch

Your whole body plays a vital role in the success of every pitch. Whether you are throwing a ball overhand or underhand, your body becomes an "instrument," producing a rhythm with all the different parts of your body working in correct sequence. That is why beginning with proper mechanics is so important. Try to picture your body going through the full motion as explained below.

1. **STANCE**
   a. Your feet should be shoulder width apart in a comfortable stance.
   b. The ball of your right foot rests on the front of the pitching rubber; the toes of your left foot rest on the back of the pitching rubber with your heel off the rubber.
   c. Your weight is distributed, with 70% on your left foot and 30% on your right foot. With that ratio, you should be able to lift up your right foot and balance on your left foot. The softball is in your pitching hand resting at the side of your body.

2. **BODY MOVEMENT**
   a. Your hands are now brought together in front of your chest (hiding the ball in your glove) to begin the windup.
   b. Your weight shifts to your right leg with shoulders slightly forward to begin your momentum towards your catcher. Your hands slide down towards your right foot, straightening your arms into the starting position of your arm circle.
   c. As your glove hand and pitching hand begin the upswing of your arm circle, your left leg, which is also known as your ***stride leg***, moves forward, striding down the ***power line*** into the ***power position.*** (Your foot is not planted yet.) The ***power line*** is an imaginary straight line which extends from the middle of the pitching rubber to home plate. The ***power position*** is your body position on the power line where your feet are at a 45-degree angle, shoulder-width apart, with your toes on the power line.

Proper Mechanics

Fig. 2.1 Power position on the power line.

d. Your right foot, known as the ***pivot foot*** since it pivots on the front of the pitching rubber, pushes hard off the pitcher's rubber (this occurs simultaneously with "c" above).
e. As your body starts forward, your left shoulder points towards home plate opening up your hips; your pitching arm continues its revolution.
f. At the top of the back swing, your left shoulder and glove hand are pointing towards home plate.
g. Your pitching arm is now next to your right ear pointing straight up in the ***line of force.*** The line of force is the circle directly next to your body which your pitching arm follows. Imagine the face of a clock next to your body, and your pitching arm circles counterclockwise. Your pitching hand begins its rotation.
h. Your shoulder and hips begin to close; your right arm stays close to your body.
i. Your right shoulder drops slightly and behind your left shoulder as you begin the downswing; your wrist is cocked and your body is upright.
j. Your left foot begins to plant with your toes slightly facing third base; your right toe is starting to drag off the pitching rubber.
k. Your left foot is planted, and your knee slightly bent.
l. Your right toe continues to drag away from pitcher's rubber, creating a "question mark" in the dirt as you push off the pitching rubber.

Diamond Girl

    m. Your shoulders and hips continue to close; your wrist is kept very close to your body with the wrist snapping slightly in front of your right leg; your arm continues the follow-through.
    n. Your right leg slides back into the power line (finishing your "question mark") as your glove hand is brought back towards your left shoulder.
    o. Your hips are now completely closed; your body is now facing the catcher and your body is in a defensive stance with your glove hand near your left shoulder.

The Grips

The fastball is the first pitch a beginner learns. The importance of the fastball grip is to create quick rotation (spin) of the ball using correct finger placement on the seams. The beginner practices using good wrist snap and getting accustomed to rolling the ball off her fingertips.

There are two grips used for throwing the fastball: the 4-seam fastball grip and the 2-seam fastball grip. The 4-seam grip produces a straighter path to the catcher. The 2-seam grip produces more movement on the ball and is more difficult to control due to wrist movement and finger release. Thus, the 2-seamer is used by the more advanced pitcher.

Fig. 2.2.a 4-seam fastball grip.   **Fig. 2.2.b** 2-seam fastball grip.

The proper grip for beginners is the 4-seam fastball grip and should be used when practicing the beginner pitching drills. When holding the ball, you need to look for the seams on the ball that resemble a "C." If

Proper Mechanics

you hold the softball with the manufacturer's insignia facing you and turn the softball clockwise about 1/4 turn, you will be able to see the "C." Your index, middle, and ring fingers are placed on the top seam, and your thumb is placed on a bottom seam, preferably two seams down if your hand is large enough to reach it. Your little finger naturally rests on the ball. Proper placement in your hand will produce a gap between the ball and your hand, and your fingers will "pull" on the seams on release when using proper wrist snap, creating a four-seam spin.

Now you're ready to start practicing!

CHAPTER 3
Wrist Snap and Release

Professional softball pitchers are capable of throwing a softball up to speeds of 60-70 miles per hour. If you watch these pitchers closely, they make pitching look effortless because their *whole* body is in complete rhythm – their arms, their legs, their hips, their shoulders, and their breathing (yes, even their breathing!). One of the most important elements is the wrist snap.

Proper wrist snap is accomplished by acquiring a loose, relaxed wrist. Good wrist snap will result in fast ball release, generating speed and spin by the pull on the seam by your fingertips. (Note: Throughout this book I mention using your "fingertips" when gripping the ball as well as feeling the ball roll off your "fingertips." Technically, you are holding the ball on the *pads* of your fingers, not on the very tips of your fingers.) If the wrist tightens, the ball will be thrown flat, resulting in no spin. For instance, take your pitching hand and shake your hand back and forth as if waving as fast as you can. Now hold a softball in your hand and do the same exercise. This exercise is a lot harder to do with a ball in your hand, so you need to develop a relaxed strong wrist in order to throw hard and fast.

The following drills will help to strengthen your wrist while reinforcing the correct release point. Left-handed pitchers can make an easy adjustment for practicing these drills by positioning their feet shoulder width apart with their right foot as the lead foot on the power line. Almost all of these drills are done from the power position on the power line. During indoor practices you may want to use lines on a gym floor as a "visual aid." Try to make the ball travel the path of this line to your catcher. You can also put a piece of masking tape on the floor to create the image of the power line. If you're practicing at a softball field, you can use either the foul lines along the side of the field or, if you are standing on the pitching rubber, you can take your foot and draw a line in the dirt from the center of the pitching rubber towards home plate. Your power position opens up your hips so that your pitching arm can easily swing past your hips down

Diamond Girl

the power line. (When we get into the full motion, you will see how your hips act like a door, opening when stepping into the power position, then closing as you pitch the ball.) Remember that the muscles, tendons, and ligaments in your arm need to be "trained" to throw the ball properly, and this does not happen overnight. Practicing these drills will reinforce basic wrist snap mechanics.

Tip: Have someone draw a "smiley face" on the palm of your pitching hand. This serves as a wonderful visual aid. If you do the wrist snap drills properly, your "smiley face" will be looking directly at you when you finish your wrist snap!

You can also have someone write the word "Hi" on the top of your hand. When you use the proper wrist snap, you will see the "smiley face" and your catcher will see the word "Hi".

Also, don't forget to stretch!

Wrist Snap Drills

(1) Arm Extension Snap Drill with Help

Mona Stevens played college softball at the University of Utah where she set almost all of the school's pitching records. She played 17 years of Women's Open Division ASA Softball, has coached all levels including collegiate softball at the University of Utah, and has been one of this country's top clinicians and instructors of softball skills. She included this drill in her book *Fastpitch Pitching Drill Book, 1993*.

Hold a softball in your pitching hand and extend your pitching hand in front of your body, palm side up, at shoulder height. Since you don't want to toss the ball with your arm, a coach/parent can support your arm using two fingers under your elbow, and two fingers resting on top of your forearm. (The coach/parent should not grab your arm as this will produce a tightened wrist snap.) The wrist is cocked and ready to toss the ball straight up in the air. Using only your wrist, toss the ball. If the wrist snap is done properly, you will feel the ball roll off your fingertips producing a lot of spin. You should see the palm of your pitching hand in front of you. You are basically "waving" to yourself. Your "smiley face" will face you when using the proper wrist snap.

Tip to coach/parent: If the young pitcher tightens up and cannot toss the ball with her wrist, the coach or parent can "be her wrist snap." Standing slightly in back of the pitcher, stretch your arm underneath hers and place your index and middle fingers under her hand. Your other fingers will *very gently* wrap around her wrist. Using your two fingers and without the ball in her hand, try to bend her hand into the ending wrist snap position. Do this a number of times to loosen her hand. Once the young pitcher's hand seems fairly loose, add the ball and help her toss the ball up in the air. The player can also toss the ball on the count of "3," using the counts of "1" and "2" as practice snaps to loosen her wrist.

Wrist Snap and Release

Fig. 3.1.a Ready position with the coach gently holding the pitcher's arm.

Fig. 3.1.b The pitcher uses her wrist snap to toss the ball, finishing with her wrist bent and able to see her palm.

Diamond Girl

(2) Arm Extension Snap Drill without Help

Now that you have mastered drill #1, try this drill by yourself without help from a coach or parent. Remember to start this drill with your pitching arm extended at shoulder height using only your wrist snap to toss the ball.

(3) Arm Extension Snap Drill from Power Position on Power Line

Start this drill from your power position on the power line. Now instead of holding the ball out in front of your body, move your pitching arm into the position where your pitching hand will be at the location of the proper release point. The location of release for your fastball will be slightly in front of your right leg for a right-handed pitcher.

The easiest way to find the correct release point is as follows: standing in your power position on the power line with your pitching arm hanging straight down at your side, rest your elbow on the side of your hip bone. Now slide your elbow forward to the point where your elbow now rests on the *front* of your hip bone. This is your correct release point. The elbow of the pitching arm should be located (and resting) just in front of the hip bone. (Note: When pitching, your elbow will always go past your hip bone. If you stop your arm directly next to your hip bone, you will actually throw the ball using your elbow instead of proper wrist snap, and you will feel your arm tighten up. This can potentially cause elbow problems. Thus, we practice this drill from proper release point, in front of the hip.) Keeping the arm in place, either by someone holding it there (hand resting on forearm) or by yourself, toss the ball to the catcher using only a wrist snap. If proper wrist snap is used, you should be able to glance down at your pitching hand and see the "smiley face."

Fig. 3.2.a The coach holds the pitcher's arm at her release point.

Fig. 3.2.b The pitcher is able to see her palm if proper wrist snap is used.

(4) Arm Extension Snap Drill with Follow-Through

Standing in your power position on the power line as in the drill above, you will now add a little follow-through to your wrist snap. Without grabbing the elbow of your pitching arm, rest your pitching elbow in the palm of your opposite hand. As you toss the ball using your wrist snap, you or your coach pushes your pitching arm towards your catcher, creating the sensation of the follow-through. The arm should be relaxed and easy to push forward. The pitching hand will end up as mentioned in Drill #1. With your arm out in front, you should see the smiley face on the palm of your pitching hand.

Fig. 3.3.a The pitcher cups her pitching elbow, keeping her thumb underneath her arm.

Fig. 3.3.b The pitching arm is pushed forward to imitate the follow-through.

(5) Hoop Drill

This drill requires the use of a small light-weight hoop or ring such as plastic rings used for games in swimming. It can be done either kneeling or standing. The use of knee pads or a pillow will greatly aid in the drill if done from the kneeling position.

Starting in a kneeling position with your left knee on the ground while your right leg is bent, rest your pitching arm on your bent right leg. Hold the hoop lightly in your hand letting your hand and hoop hang towards the floor. Using only your wrist, snap your wrist so that the hoop flips up and rests on your forearm.

Diamond Girl

(6) Rainbow Drill

Stand in a "T" position with arms extended at shoulder height and with the ball in your pitching hand. Use only your wrist snap and toss the ball over your head, creating a "rainbow." Catch the ball in your glove hand. Note: you must **watch** the ball starting in your pitching hand all the way to your glove hand or you won't catch the ball. Keep your eye on the ball from one hand to the other.

Fig. 3.4.a Starting "T" position.　　　　　　　**Fig. 3.4.b** Toss the ball over your head.

If you're having problems using only your wrist snap, a coach/parent can be your wrist snap again as in drill #1. Start in your "T" position as mentioned above. Your coach/parent stands behind you with their arm stretched out underneath your arm. The coach/parent places their index and middle fingers under your hand. Their other fingers will *very gently* wrap around your wrist. Your coach/parent will help you to toss the ball up and over your head creating a rainbow. Your elbow may bend slightly, but you want the coach/parent to prevent your arm from going above your head when tossing the ball.

Fig. 3.4.c Keep your eye on the ball as it travels over your head and into your glove.

If you still have problems getting the ball to go over your head but you are using the correct mechanics (wrist snap, getting a lot of spin on the ball by the ball rolling off your fingertips), don't panic. As your wrist gets stronger, you will have no problem completing this drill.

(7) Under Knee Drill

If there is only one drill that the young pitcher has time to do each day, this is the one! This drill is another favorite of mine from Mona Stevens' book *Fastpitch Pitching Drill Book, 1993*. This drill, done from a sitting position on the floor, really helps to strengthen the wrist. You can build up the number of reps, beginning with 25-30 reps (less for very young pitchers). More advanced pitchers can start with 50-150 reps, and they can also use weighted softballs.

Sit on the floor. For right-handed pitchers, your left foot is placed next to your right knee. Your pitching hand, while holding the ball, goes under your knee. Your knee acts as a barrier. Toss the ball straight up in the air using your wrist snap and catch the ball with your other hand. If you use proper wrist snap, you will "catch" your leg, resting your hand near your knee upon release of the ball. Catch the ball with your other hand in order to complete your wrist snap and catch your leg.

Fig. 3.5.a Place your pitching hand underneath your knee. Some pitchers prefer to rest their pitching hand on the ground to begin this drill.

Fig. 3.5.b "Catch" your leg to finish your wrist snap.

(8) Framing the Pitch

The main objective of the framing drill is to focus on the wrist snap, release point, and follow-through by breaking down the arm circle into smaller segments, or frames, and then building on the previous frame. Imagine taking sequential photographs of a pitcher's arm circle as she is throwing the ball. In one frame you would see her arm at one point in her arm circle, the next frame her arm would be a little further, and so on. This drill is one you will want to use in your practices or warm-up time before a game.

This drill can be done in a kneeling or standing position. Since our focus is on the wrist snap and arm swing and not on the legs and hips just yet, beginner pitchers are encouraged to practice from the kneeling position until the mechanics are sound. Keep your arm relaxed so that it can swing freely using your wrist snap at the proper point of release. Your elbow continues past your hip, and you finish with your follow-through, seeing the palm of your hand out in front of you.

Your glove hand also plays a vital role in pitching. Not only does your glove hand stop the balls hit back at you, but your glove hand helps to rotate your upper body. As you do the framing drills below, keep in mind that as your pitching hand comes forward towards your catcher, your glove hand comes back

Wrist Snap and Release

towards your left shoulder, open wide with fingers pointing towards the sky, in a ready position to catch the ball.

Start in a kneeling position with your body positioned on the power line in the power position. Your right knee is on the power line; your left foot (big toe) is extended down the power line for balance.

¼ Frame: Your hands start in a "T" position with your glove hand pointing towards your catcher and your pitching hand extended behind your body down the power line with your wrist cocked. Relax and let your arm swing, releasing the ball just in front of your right leg, finishing with a nice easy follow-through. You should see the palm of your hand and the catcher should see the back of your hand. Don't forget that glove hand! Bring it back towards your shoulder to help rotate your body as well as getting you ready to catch the ball.

Fig. 3.6.a Start from a kneeling position in order to focus on the wrist snap at the proper release point.

Fig. 3.6.b All framing drills will finish with your follow-through.

½ Frame: Use the same kneeling position, but start with your pitching arm above your head next to your ear and your glove hand pointing toward your catcher. Follow the finishing directions for ¼ frame drill.

Diamond Girl

Fig. 3.6.c Starting position for ½ frame. **Fig. 3.6.d** Starting position for ¾ frame.

¾ Frame: Use the same kneeling position, but start with both hands pointing towards your catcher. Follow the finishing directions as stated above.

Full frame: Use the same kneeling position, but start with both hands slightly in front of your kneeling leg. Follow the same finishing directions as above (see Fig. 3.6.e).

Advanced Pitchers – Framing Drill from a Standing Position:
Advanced pitchers stand on the power line in the power position with their feet shoulder width apart and stationary at the start of each frame indicated above. Your front (stride) foot steps down the power line approximately 4 inches on the downswing of your pitching arm. As your pitching arm passes the hip, snap your wrist and rotate your hip, remembering that your glove hand comes back to your shoulder while your pitching arm follows through. End with the knee on your pitching hand side pointing down the power line to your catcher. You need to pivot on the ball of your foot. Your hips are now facing your catcher.

Wrist Snap and Release

Fig. 3.6.e Starting position for full frame.

(9) Soup Can Drill

The purpose of this drill is to simulate the "feel" of the ball rolling off your fingers, producing the correct fastball spin. You need a soup can for this drill. You will actually be pitching the can to your catcher so do not throw hard. Also, do not use a can with a pull tab on the top as the ingredients will begin to leak if the can is dropped several times.

You will need a can that has an even weight to it, such as a can of cream of chicken soup (for pitchers with small hands) or a can of pumpkin (for pitchers with larger hands). Kneel or stand in the ¼ Framing Drill position and hold the can horizontally. Then *gently* throw the can so that it remains horizontal. If the can rolls off your fingers correctly, it will have an even spin to it like a car tire. If the can did not roll off your fingers properly the can will have a "wiggle" to it.

(10) Pitch to Yourself

Start by standing on the power line in your power position. Hold your glove 4-6 inches in front of your release point and practice pitching to yourself. Use your full arm circle, snapping the ball into your glove

Diamond Girl

with your wrist, and following through with your pitching arm. Remember that your follow through includes your elbow going past your hip, and the palm of your pitching hand ending up in front of your face. You should be able to see the palm of your hand – see your "smiley face."

(11) <u>Bent Leg Pitching</u>

This drill takes a little more practice if your wrist is still a bit weak, but it is another great drill to improve your wrist strength. Since this drill is done from a kneeling position, it completely isolates the wrist.

Start by straddling the power line. Drop to a kneeling position, still straddling the power line with your knees. Your left knee rests on the floor parallel to the power line while your right knee is bent and extended vertically to the power line. Start with both hands resting along the inside of your left knee. Your glove hand and pitching hand come up together as you start your pitch. Your glove hand stops at the position where it points towards your catcher. Your pitching arm continues through the arm circle and, using your wrist snap, you throw the ball *under* your bent leg. You will know if you used proper wrist snap because your hand will "catch" the underside of your thigh.

Fig. 3.7.a Your right leg is bent and horizontal to the ground.

Wrist Snap and Release

Fig. 3.7.b Finish by catching the underside of your leg to complete your wrist snap.

CHAPTER 4
The Arm Circle

The arm circle creates velocity. The more relaxed the arm, the faster the arm speed. For instance, standing in your power position and without a softball in your hand, relax your pitching arm and do ten arm circles in a row as fast as you can. This is the arm speed you want to achieve. Great softball pitchers have the ability to literally "cut themselves in half" with the upper body being relaxed while the lower body (legs and hips) is driving and forceful. Their pitching arm remains close to their body throughout the arm circle in the line of force.

Let's focus on the movement of the arm as it goes through the arm circle. Stand in the power position on the power line as you previously did in the Full Frame Wrist Snap drill in Chapter 3. With both hands relaxed and resting on the right side of the left leg, the pitching hand and glove hand separate as they start their upswing. The glove hand points towards your catcher. The pitching hand follows the power line with the back of the hand facing the catcher.

As the hand continues towards the top of the arm circle, the wrist begins to turn outwards while the arm stays in the line of force and positioned next to your ear. The arm is extended (reaching towards the sky) and the softball is held on your fingertips as far away from your body as possible. As you begin the downswing of your arm circle, your wrist will continue to rotate, getting into a cocked wrist position. Your arm continues through the downswing with your wrist cocked. Once it reaches the release point (slightly in front of your right leg), your wrist snaps, releasing the ball.

Diamond Girl

Arm Circle Drills

(1) Coach-assisted Circles

This drill helps you get the feel of the fully-extended arm throughout the arm circle and is done with the aid of a parent/coach. Stand in your power position with your pitching arm next to your side. The coach will face your pitching hand side. Grasping your hand from the *underside* (palm to palm), the coach extends your arm through the arm circle, ending the circle by *throwing* your hand out into the follow-through. Start by doing this drill slowly. Then increase to a smooth, rhythmic speed.

Fig. 4.1.a Stand in your power position to begin this drill.

Fig. 4.1.b Your arm is extended throughout the arm circle.

The Arm Circle

Fig. 4.1.c Focus on the feeling of your arm extension throughout the arm circle, finishing with the follow-through.

(2) <u>Wall Arm Circles</u>

This drill helps you keep your arm throughout the line of force. Your arm should be kept next to your body in the line of force for maximum power. Since you are focusing on mechanics, do not pitch fast but focus on your arm swing.

Kneel (for beginners) or stand (for more advanced students) only a few inches away from the wall in your power position on the power line, allowing just enough room for you to swing your pitching arm. You and your catcher should be fairly close, about 20 feet apart. Using the framing drill indicated above, pitch the ball to your catcher. Your upper body will rotate to face your catcher as your glove hand moves back towards your shoulder. Your pitching hand stays close to your body and follows the path next to the wall as you pitch. If your arm leaves the line of force, your arm and/or elbow will bump into the wall.

Diamond Girl

Fig. 4.2.a Your stance is on the power line close to a wall or fence.

Fig. 4.2.b Finish the pitch with your follow-through – see your "smiley face."

(3) <u>Trash Bag Circles</u>

This drill, like the Coach-assisted Circles, will also help you feel the extension needed in the arm circle. Put three or four softballs in a plastic double-bagged grocery bag and tie the ends together so the balls do not fly out. Holding onto the tied end, swing the bag using your full arm circle while standing in your power position. The weight of the balls in the bag will extend your arm. Once you get the feel of this, throw the bag of balls using your wrist snap at release point, trying to throw the bag into a wall or to your catcher, similar to a line drive.

For a fun summer version of this drill, use a small bucket filled halfway with water instead of the bag of balls. Swing the bucket using your full arm circle, keeping the bucket in the line of force. The bucket will extend your arm. If you slow your arm speed, you will get wet!

(4) Point to the Target Drill

This drill corrects the problem of the follow-through of your pitching arm moving *across* your body and out of the line of force. Stand in your power position and, using your full wind-up, pitch the ball using your wrist snap and *point* in the direction of your target after your follow-through. If your follow-through carried your pitching arm across your body, you will have to bring your arm back into the line of force in order to point to your target.

CHAPTER 5
The Hip Turn

Pitchers generate a great deal of power by using strong hips and legs. If pitchers throw the ball with all arm motion, in time they will develop shoulder and arm problems. Since girls don't have the same upper body strength as boys, girls need to utilize their hips and legs as much as possible.

One key element to remember as mentioned earlier – your elbow will always go past your hip before you close your hip. As you release the ball, your right hip will rotate hard. In other words, we say "throw the ball with your hip" so that your body is now completely facing your catcher. Almost all of the pitcher's power is generated from her hips and legs, so she needs a good hard hip turn.

Your glove hand plays a vital role in your hip turn. As your pitching hand continues into the follow-through, your glove hand is pulled back towards your left shoulder. This motion produces rotation of your upper body and right hip. (Remember the follow-through requires you to see the palm of your hand in front of you, and your catcher needs to see the back of your hand.) In other words, you are using opposite forces to propel the softball. Your glove hand is now near your shoulder, ready to catch the ball and protect your face if it's hit back at you.

Here are a few drills that will help to "throw your hips" into the pitch.

(1) Glove Pull

This drill is done with the assistance of a coach or parent. Stand in your power position on the power line and extend your glove hand out towards your coach. The coach holds onto your glove, giving some resistance, as you try to "pull" your coach past your body. Do not move your feet. As you pull with your arm, you also utilize your hips to turn as you pull. Your hips end up square facing your catcher.

Diamond Girl

Fig. 5.1.a The coach holds your glove, giving resistance as you pull.

Fig. 5.1.b Pull the glove by turning your hips. Your upper body automatically turns and you finish in correct position facing your catcher.

(2) "Squish the Bug"

This drill may seem familiar because it is similar to a batting drill. Batters use this drill to practice using their hips to add more power in hitting the ball. Pitchers use this drill to practice using their hips to add power to the pitch.

Stand in your power position on the power line. Without moving your front foot, pivot on your back (*pivot*) foot, ending with your hips facing your catcher. Your hips are square, and the knee of your pivot foot is pointing down the power line to your catcher. Eighty-five percent of your weight should still be resting on your back (pivot) foot.

(3) Holding Arm Drill

This drill is more difficult and it takes some time to get used to it, but it helps you learn the feel of the movement of the hips. Standing in the power position on the power line and without your glove, place

The Hip Turn

your left arm behind your back. With the palm of your left hand facing outward, place your left hand under your pitching arm just above the elbow. It is important that you continue to hold onto your pitching arm throughout the drill.

Fig. 5.2.a Stand in your power position holding your upper right arm and weight on back leg.

Holding the ball in your pitching hand, shift your weight to your back (pivot) foot and extend your pitching hand down the power line behind you as you did in the ¼ frame drill. Your wrist should be cocked and ready to throw the ball. Make sure your pitching hand is on the power line and not wrapped around your back. This will cause you to sling the ball out to the side.

Start by taking a small step about 2-4 inches with your stride foot down the power line. At the same time, start your pitching motion (still holding onto your right arm with your left hand). Throw the ball using your wrist snap, and finish with your hips facing your catcher. In order for you to get the ball to your catcher, you must snap your hips to end up square to your catcher or the ball will be thrown out to your right and not down the power line.

Diamond Girl

Fig. 5.2.b Pivot on your back foot to turn your hips.

(4) Glove-to-Wall Drill

Start this drill by standing on a pretend pitching rubber with a staggered stance and facing the wall approximately 7-8 feet away from the wall. (Note: you will not be throwing a ball in this drill but going through your full motion.) Using your full motion, extend your glove hand towards the wall, turning your hips and standing in your power position. Continue your pitching motion with your pitching hand extending towards the wall on your follow-through as your glove hand comes back to your shoulder. Do this several times to get the feel of the glove hand "pulling" you towards the wall.

(5) Knee Lift Drill

This drill really utilizes the hips, incorporating more power and speed into the pitch. It should be used by a pitcher with fairly good mechanics who wants to increase her speed.

Start in the ¼ frame position as you did in the standing framing drill mentioned in the section "The Wrist Snap." Your glove hand points toward your target and your pitching hand is parallel to the ground with your wrist cocked. Your feet are on the power line in your power position, but with one exception –

The Hip Turn

you now start with a **wide** stance, meaning your feet are twice the width of your regular stance. Your knees should be slightly flexed with your weight on your back foot. Begin your pitch by relaxing your pitching arm, letting it swing forward while your glove hand comes back towards your left shoulder, helping to turn your upper body. Your shoulders will lean slightly back and behind your release point. This is the correct shoulder position for the fast ball. As you square your hips and release the ball, you follow through not only with your pitching hand but also with the knee of your pivot foot, bringing your knee up as if marching, and returning it to the ground slightly behind your body. (You basically fall back on your foot.) You will notice that your knee is in direct line with your catcher. Using your knee forces you to turn your hips.

Continue this drill using ½ frame, ¾ frame, and full frame.

Fig. 5.3.a Start with a wide stance and weight on the back leg.

Fig. 5.3.b Your knee follows your pitching hand. Your front foot acts as a brace, forcing your shoulders to stay slightly back and behind your release point.

Fig. 5.3.c Your pivot foot finishes back on the power line.

CHAPTER 6
Balance

Imagine you are walking across stepping stones leading to the other side of a small creek. You steady yourself so as not to fall into the water. Or, remember your first attempt at riding a bicycle without training wheels? It was more difficult than you expected. You swerved left and right as you desperately tried to stay on line.

Now picture the tennis player who is serving the ball at the beginning of a match. She tosses the ball high in the air while bringing her racket behind her body, arching her back, then leaping into the air while thrusting her body and racket forward hitting the ball with extreme force. Picture the golfer who is about to drive the ball down the fairway. She gets into her proper stance with the club nestled next to the ball on the tee. She swings the club back and above her shoulders while rotating her body in order to get into position to drive through the ball with extreme force. Or what about the gymnast who not only walks down the beam with ease but completes somersaults as well, landing solidly on the beam?

Everyday people as well as athletes rely on good balance in order to prevent themselves from falling, miss-hitting the ball, or falling off the balance beam. Softball pitchers also need good balance in order to get their bodies in the proper position to maximize their power.

Here are a few drills which will help with balance.

(1) The Rocker Drill

This drill is done from a kneeling position on the power line in the power position and it helps you get the feel of your shoulders leaning slightly back. Your shoulders will always be slightly behind your release point. Your right knee will be on the power line with your left foot extended down the power line for

Diamond Girl

balance (similar to the starting position for the framing drill). From this position, practice "rocking" forward with your upper body and then pushing your upper body back using your front leg.

Now add your hands. Your hands are together dangling between your legs with the ball in your glove hand. As you rock forward, your pitching hand starts its upswing while your left forearm rests on your left leg. You can also reach your glove hand towards your catcher if you would like. As you begin your downswing with your arm, push back with your front leg, forcing your shoulders to go back. Continue with the release of the ball and a nice comfortable follow-through with your pitching arm (your shoulders will be slightly behind your release point). If it helps, you can count to "3" while performing this drill since there are three steps in this rocker drill -- ("1") hands dangling in the starting position; ("2") rock forward resting your left forearm (glove hand) on your knee and pitching hand starting the upswing; and ("3") shoulders are pushed back using your front leg while your pitching arm is on the downswing, following with the release of the ball and follow-through.

Fig. 6.1.a Your right knee is on the power line while your left foot is extended down the power line.

Fig. 6.1.b As your pitching arm begins its circle, your upper body leans slightly forward.

Balance

Fig. 6.1.c Your front foot pushes your shoulders back.

Diamond Girl

(2) Bucket Balance Drill

Using the same principles as in the Rocker Drill, stand in your power position on your power line, but this time your front stride foot rests gently on the edge of an upside-down bucket. This position keeps your shoulders and weight back. Using your full pitching arm motion, throw the ball to your catcher. If your weight shifts forward causing you to lose your balance, the bucket will be pushed forward, resulting in your stride foot falling to the ground.

Fig. 6.2.a Stand in your power position with your left foot on the edge of a bucket.

Fig. 6.2.b Keep your foot on the bucket, turning your hips and pivoting on your pivot foot.

Balance

(3) Balance Beam Drill

This drill works on keeping your balance while standing on a beam. The use of the beam will reinforce your body position as you stride towards your catcher.

Have your parent or coach place a 2"x4"x4' board on the ground. This "balance beam" will be your power line. Stand on the board in your power position being careful not to fall. Practice the framing drill mentioned in Chapter 3 while balancing on the beam. Remember to pivot on your pivot foot so that your hips face your catcher upon release of the ball.

Fig. 6.3.a Stand in your power position on the beam, getting your balance before pitching the ball.

Fig. 6.3.b Pivot on your pivot foot, ending with your right knee pointing down the beam towards your catcher.

CHAPTER 7
The Stride

Beginners should think about pitching as "walking towards your catcher." You have a natural rhythm to your body as you walk – your arms are relaxed and swing by your side. You also have a natural hip turn as you walk. When you pitch, your pitching arm should be relaxed throughout the arm circle to create velocity. Your hip turn, though, becomes exaggerated and "open" like a door as you stride down the power line. Your hips finish their motion by "closing" the door, utilizing not only your hips but also the large muscles in your legs to generate power.

Walking towards your catcher is fine when you are practicing to get all your mechanics working together. But walking is not going to give you the necessary power and explosiveness off the pitching mound. A short stride takes speed off the pitch and forces the pitcher to use more arm than leg drive. A short stride also tends to throw the body off balance. Too much leg drive will produce a crow-hop (replanting of the pivot foot) or a leap (pitcher jumps forward to gain momentum), both of which are illegal. As mentioned earlier in the book, your upper body needs to be relaxed and loose while your lower body needs to be driving and forceful. In other words, the stride needs to be aggressive but in control with the upper body balanced and powerful, utilizing the large muscles of your legs and hips.

The stride foot needs to land on the power line. If your stride is off line, proper rotation of your arm will also be affected, causing your arm circle to also be off line.

Here are a few drills that not only are fun but also keep your body relaxed as you practice striding towards your catcher. Start out by *walking* through the drills and then increasing the speed of your walk and

Diamond Girl

length of your stride. As your fundamentals improve, your stride will lengthen and become more aggressive naturally, and you will find yourself throwing harder.

(1) Walking Drill

This drill is one of my students' favorites and it can be done indoors around the perimeter of a gym or outside down the length of a field. You will need the help of a catcher. Remember to focus on your mechanics and getting into a rhythm with your body.

Start by facing your catcher about 25 feet apart. Using your full windup, walk towards your catcher while pitching the ball as your catcher walks backwards. Keep your body relaxed. Remember to keep walking, and do not stop. Your catcher throws the ball back to you while continuing to walk backwards. You continue to walk towards your catcher getting into position to pitch the ball again. Make sure you are pitching off your pivot foot as you continue your walk. Your hips turn your body into the power position and you follow through with your arm swing, closing your hips.

As you get comfortable with this drill, walk a little faster. Your arm swing will begin to get faster as you keep your body relaxed.

(2) Cone Drill

This drill ensures that your first step with your stride foot is on the power line. You will need two items that can be used as barriers such as two buckets or two cones.

Draw a power line in the dirt towards your catcher. Place one cone on each side of the power line approximately one foot *before* the point where you finish your stride. Pitch the ball, stepping down the power line between the cones. The cones force you to open your hips as you stride through the opening. Your pivot foot follows through the opening forcing your hips to close. Both feet finish in front of the cones.

The Stride

Fig. 7.1.a Cones are placed along the power line.

Fig. 7.1.b Step through the cones, opening your hips.

Fig. 7.1.c Finish with both feet in front of the cones.

Diamond Girl

(3) <u>Three-Step Walking Drill</u>

This drill improves body rhythm and momentum towards your catcher from the pitcher's rubber. Counting "1", "2", "3" and "go" to yourself will aid in this drill.

Stand on the pitchers rubber and take three steps back. As in the pre-motion, your glove and pitching hands start together, chest high. Begin with your pivot foot and take two steps ("1", "2") towards the pitcher's rubber. With your *third* step ("3"), your pivot foot needs to land on the front of the pitching rubber. This is the most important step as it gets you in a position to use an aggressive push-off from the rubber. Use your full windup and pitch the ball pushing hard off the pitching rubber ("go"). As you get comfortable with this drill, try walking faster!

CHAPTER 8
Pitching from the Pitching Rubber

The goal of a pitcher is to produce one fluidic motion while creating maximum power. Up to this point the focus has been on individual components of the actual pitch. The pitch itself starts from the pitching rubber with what is called the "pre-motion."

The pre-motion begins with your stance on the pitching rubber. If you refer back to Chapter 2," Basic Fundamentals of the Pitch," you step onto the pitching rubber with your right foot first, positioning the ball of your foot in contact with the front of the pitching rubber. The toes of your left foot rest on the back of the pitching rubber. Your feet should be about shoulder width apart in a comfortable stance and within the confines of the left and right edges of the rubber. If your stance is too wide, you will find yourself rocking to your right in order to shift your weight to your right leg causing your body to go off balance.

Your glove hand and pitching hand holding the ball hang naturally at your sides. Once your feet are placed and your body is in position using the correct weight distribution with 70% on your left, or stride, foot and 30% on your right, or pivot, foot, your hands come together in front of your chest, hiding the ball in your glove. You are now in position to start your full motion.

Your weight begins to shift to your pivot foot as your shoulders lean slightly forward to begin your momentum towards your catcher. Your hands slide down towards your right foot, as you straighten your arms into the starting position of your arm circle. As a visual aid, picture a sliding board directly in front of you. You want your hands to follow the sliding board with your hands going down the slide and finishing towards your catcher. As you finish your slide, your pitching hand continues on its upswing as your glove hand stops parallel to the ground with your left shoulder pointing towards your catcher.

As your momentum continues forward, your stride leg steps onto the power line getting your body into your power position. If someone were to take a picture of you at this point, your body would be in a

Diamond Girl

position which looks similar to the letter "K." (You are in your "super K" position.) Your pitching hand continues through its downswing as your right foot begins to push hard off the pitching rubber. Your glove hand comes back to your left shoulder as you release the ball. Your right hip comes through, "closing the door," as you continue your toe drag and follow through with your pitching hand. Your right foot will slide up the power line and then step out into a defensive stance.

CHAPTER 9
Location! Location! Location!

The basic strike zone consists of an imaginary area extending from the batter's armpits to the knees and within the confines of the dimension of home plate. However, there are other strike zones to consider. One is the pitcher's strike zone. That is where the pitcher works the corners of the plate keeping the ball out of the area the batter prefers. Another is the batter's strike zone. The batter looks for balls entering the area of the strike zone where she can hit the ball solidly. Finally is the umpire's strike zone. Some umpires prefer lower pitches and will call more strikes in this area while some prefer higher pitches. It is up to the pitcher to adapt to the umpire's strike zone, realizing where he/she consistently calls strikes and working around that. Of course, the one strike zone you try to avoid is the batter's strike zone!

A ball that is thrown high or low to one of the corners of the plate or out of the strike zone over the middle of the plate is harder to hit than "a meatball" thrown down the heart of the plate. A ball pitched right down the middle of the plate will probably end up over your outfielder's head or over the outfield fence for a home run.

A pitcher's best pitched game is one where she *appears* to be throwing strikes but, in reality, is actually throwing the ball just off the corners of the plate. For instance, if a right-handed batter is up to bat and she is standing close to home plate, you want to throw a high or low pitch close to her, forcing her to weakly hit the ball off the handle of the bat. You are forcing the batter to hit the pitch you want her to hit. You are forcing the batter to reach for the ball instead of easily swinging the bat on a flat plane.

Pitchers focus on six locations surrounding the strike zone: 1) low inside, 2) high inside, 3) low outside, 4) high outside, 5) low middle, and 6) high middle. Pitchers try to stay away from middle inside and middle outside as the batter's swing would be directly on the plane of the path of the ball.

Diamond Girl

For young pitchers, your coach may give you or your catcher a signal of where he/she wants the pitch to be thrown. As you become more experienced, you will learn to pick up clues from the batter as to which location or pitch she may or may not like to hit. Clues include her stance, the way she swings her bat in warm-ups in the batter's box, as well as the way she holds her bat.

It takes a lot of practice and discipline to consistently hit the corners of the plate where your catcher sets up her glove for the pitch. Practicing the wrist snap drills and reinforcing the release point will help to improve your accuracy.

Before you begin the following accuracy drills, you need to remember three elements before throwing each pitch:

1. Think about the mechanics of the pitch. For instance, am I holding the ball correctly? Where is my release point? Should my stride be long or short?
2. Visualize the path of the ball. Visualization is a key factor in producing accuracy. You need to think about the path the ball needs to travel from your release point to your catcher's glove. If you've ever watched a replay of a golf putt on T.V., the media will use a dotted line showing the path of the ball from the club to the hole. Mentally you need to do the same in softball. Try to visualize a path of softballs beginning from your release point and ending in your catcher's glove.
3. Clear your mind. Now that you have gone over the mechanics and visualization in your mind, it's time to throw the ball. Clear your mind of everything and just throw it.

Spot Pitching

Pitchers of all levels constantly practice spot pitching because they know how important it is to have control of the batter. Your job is to force the batter to either strike out or hit a pitch that will produce a fly ball or a ground ball for an out. At times you will face batters that seem to hit everything. Keep in mind that batters always have one weakness – a specific pitch or specific location where they can't hit the ball solidly. You just need to find it.

When you practice spot pitching either with a catcher or by yourself you still need to step down a power line which is either drawn in the dirt if you're at a field or made from tape if you're in a gym. All the drills you have practiced up to this point forced you to throw the pitch directly down the middle to your catcher. You also need to master pitching to the corners of the plate since it is harder for a batter to hit these pitches. You still need to step down a power line. For example, if you are throwing to your catcher who is positioned on the inside corner to a right-handed batter, your power line is angled such that it extends from the pitching rubber to your catcher's glove. *Your first step, or stride, will always go down a power line towards your catcher's glove, no matter where she positions it*. This will open up your hips keeping your pitching mechanics the same as when you practiced, keeping your body in the power position and your feet on the power line. Remember to visualize the path of the ball before throwing it.

Location! Location! Location!

As you do these drills, keep a bucket of balls handy so you don't have to keep chasing the ball each time you pitch.

(1) Spot Pitching To a Catcher

Have your catcher position her glove at the six locations. Using your full pitching motion, try to throw three to five pitches to one location before moving onto the next location. You will notice that your release point and shoulder position will slightly change as you throw to the various locations. For instance, if you are throwing at a high target, your release point will be slightly forward of your normal release point while your shoulders lean slightly back. Your stride will always be down the power line towards your catcher's glove.

(2) Spot Pitching to a Target on a Wall

If you don't have someone to catch for you, you can still practice this drill by using a number of different ways. You can draw the locations on a piece of cardboard and hang it on the wall. You can also use pieces of tape and mark an "X" at each location on a wall or on a garage door. For indoor practice, use a bucket of softie softballs. These are balls specifically made so that they won't damage gym floors or walls. Stand 20 feet from your target and pitch the ball trying to hit each mark. Once you are fairly accurate in hitting the targets from 20 feet, increase the distance a few feet at a time until you reach your regular pitching distance.

(3) Softball on a Cone

This is a fun drill if you have access to a cone, such as the ones used in gym class. Have someone rest a softball on the top of the cone. Pitch the ball and see how many times you can knock the ball off the cone hitting only the softball and not the cone. If you hit the cone, it does not count.

(4) Cone Batters

This drill uses cones to simulate batters and is a great pre-season tune-up for locating pitches. Place a cone in the batter's box for a right-handed batter. Have your catcher place her glove at the various pitch locations. See how many times you can hit her glove at each spot. Now transfer the cone to the left-handed batter's box and practice the same. To make the drill a little harder, place a cone in *both* batters' boxes and throw between the cones. Try to forget the cones are there and focus only on your catcher's glove. You should have no problem in game situations pitching to your catcher with live batters standing at the plate.

CHAPTER 10
Relaxation and Speed

A misconception many pitchers have is that if you tighten your pitching arm you will be able to throw faster. Without using a softball, tighten up your arm as much as possible and swing your arm through the arm circle. You will feel a lot of stress on your shoulder, moving your arm almost robotically, as you try to circle your arm. Most pitchers who tighten up their pitching arm also throw the ball using their elbow instead of their wrist. The upswing of their arm tends to be slower forcing the pitcher to "whip" the ball by stopping her arm swing next to her hip and throwing the ball with their elbow. This "whipping" motion puts a great deal of stress on the elbow.

Now close your eyes and relax your arm taking it through the arm circle as fast as you can and finishing up with your natural follow-through of your pitching hand. The stress on your shoulders has dissipated since your arm is completely relaxed. You can now swing your arm quickly through the arm circle, following through with your wrist snap.

Learning how to relax your arm is difficult. Here are a few drills which may help you relax your arm.

(1) Humming Drill

A lot of coaches use this drill to help relax your whole body while having some fun. Think of times when you were happy, such as making a favorite craft or walking on the beach and you found yourself humming. Remember how relaxed you were while humming and enjoying yourself. This drill works that same concept. If you have a CD player handy, put on your favorite music and hum along as you practice pitching! If not, hum a song you like. Just hum!

(2) 5-Second Tension Drill

Tighten up your entire body and hold it for 5 seconds. Then, relax your body releasing the tension and immediately pitch the ball.

(3) Puppet Arms Drill

You are going to pretend to be a puppet in this drill. While holding the ball in your pitching hand, lean forward with your arms dangling and your head forward. You, the "puppet," now need to come to life. Snap your body into your upward position and, using your full motion, pitch the ball. Focus on the feeling of your arms staying loose throughout the arm circle, just like they felt as the puppet.

Increasing Speed

Your catcher gives you the signal for a fastball relying on you to throw the ball with extreme velocity. The combination of relaxation and speed produces velocity. Possessing the ability to relax your arm *and* circle your arm at a tremendous speed takes practice.

You have already practiced relaxation drills as mentioned above. You now need to incorporate speed by acquiring a quick revolution of your arm. You also need to use the explosiveness of your legs and hips to drive hard and forceful towards your catcher.

Another key element is the use of your breathing. Just as the weightlifter exhales to lift extremely heavy weights, you also want to use a good breathing technique. You may hear other pitchers "grunting" as they pitch the ball. You don't necessarily have to grunt, but you do want to exhale as you release the ball. Breathing helps your entire body utilize a relaxed rhythm. You will find yourself throwing faster with less effort.

The following speed drills will put all necessary components together and should be done when you are tired - at the end of practice - in order to help build stamina and endurance.

(1) 3 Revolutions (into a wall or a net)

Stand in your power position on the power line facing a wall or net. If you are throwing against a wall, stand back far enough from the wall so that you can catch the ball as it bounces back. The softball is in your pitching hand and your pitching arm is relaxed and loose. Without throwing the ball, quickly swing your arm through your arm circle twice. On the third revolution throw the ball as hard as you can, using a good wrist snap and a quick hard hip turn. Your pivot foot slides up into a defensive stance. Your body now faces the wall. Your glove hand should be in position to catch the ball as it comes off the wall.

Relaxation and Speed

(2) Rapid Fire Drill

This drill is also called the Speed Drill. It is very tiring but is quite effective in building stamina and arm speed. Have your catcher stand at a distance equal to the distance from the pitching mound to home plate. Pretend the softball is a hot potato and you want to get rid of it as fast as possible. Quickly pitch the softball underhand using your full motion to your catcher, keeping your arm relaxed. Immediately return to your starting location before your catcher throws the ball back to you. Avoid the tendency to move closer to your catcher instead of moving back to your original position.

The important thing with this drill is to keep the action going. As soon as your catcher catches the ball, she throws it right back to you. When you catch it, immediately throw it back to your catcher. Pitch 10 pitches in a row as fast as possible. Work up to 3 sets of 10 pitches with a thirty-second break between sets.

(3) 3-Ball Drill

This drill helps to get your whole body into a comfortable, relaxed motion. Do this drill slowly at first until you get used to the motion. As you get accustomed to the mechanics, you can start to increase the speed between pitches.

Start with two softballs. Hold one ball in your pitching hand and the other one in your glove hand. Your catcher holds a third ball in her throwing hand.

Throw the ball in your pitching hand to your catcher. Immediately transfer the ball from your glove hand to your pitching hand. Your catcher throws her ball back to you so that you are now holding two balls again. Repeat this sequence starting slowly adding more speed as you and your catcher get used to this drill.

(4) Distance Pitching

Pitching from a short distance is easy. Pitching from longer distances requires a lot of leg drive, a relaxed arm, and a good wrist snap as you will see in this drill.

Start from your normal pitching distance on the pitching mound. Pitch one or two pitches from this distance and then take two steps back. Pitch two from this distance and take two more steps back. Continue this sequence until you get to the point where you can't reach your catcher and have to bounce the ball to her.

Go back onto the pitching mound and throw 10 fast balls in a row. Throwing from this distance will now seem easy!

CHAPTER 11
Tips and Tricks for Beginners

Becoming a good pitcher doesn't happen overnight. Here are some key points to keep in mind.

1) ***Start with good mechanics***. You need to have a good foundation of basics on which to build.
2) ***Have patience!*** One thing a pitcher learns is patience. It takes a lot of repetitions to train your muscles on developing a fluid motion in order to create consistency with your pitches.
3) ***Think positive.*** Stay away from negative words such as "I can't do this." If you throw a bad pitch, forget it. Think about how to make a correction with your next pitch. Review your mechanics in your mind. Pat yourself on your back when you make a great pitch and try to remember how you did it.
4) ***Don't be afraid to take constructive criticism.*** It will help make you a better pitcher and player.
5) ***The key word is practice!*** There are always ways to practice, even if it's while you are sitting on your couch watching TV. You can hold a softball in your hand and practice feeling the correct grip, feeling the seams on your fingers, and tossing it up in the air to see how much spin you can get on the ball.

<u>*Ways you can learn about pitching*</u>:

1) ***Find a qualified pitching instructor***. Talk to pitchers who have good mechanics and ask how they learned to pitch and who taught them. If it is a male pitching coach, you need to be aware that a lot of male pitching coaches teach *men's* pitching where they don't use their hips and legs as much as a girl needs to since men possess more upper body strength. There are a lot of good male and female pitching coaches out there.

Diamond Girl

2) ***Watch video tapes and read books on softball.*** There are a lot of great tips in these to improve your game.
3) ***Watch actual competitive softball games***. Check your local newspaper to see if there are any games or tournaments being played in your locale. There are many age brackets of competition, ranging from 10&under and 12&under, through the college level. You can learn a great deal from observing other pitchers. Watch the quickness of their arm speed and the forcefulness of their leg drive. Watch where they release the ball and how they set up batters.
4) ***Imitate … to a point***. Imitation gives one the opportunity to experiment with various pitching styles in order to develop her own unique style. Study the motion of several successful pitchers and you will find that their success begins with simple mechanics. Simple mechanics not only eliminates the possibility of injuries but allows you to put all your energy into throwing the ball, not into extraneous motions.

For instance, maybe you have seen a pitcher who bends at her waist touching her glove to the ground to begin her windup. Doing this for seven or more innings not only hurts her back but expends a great deal of energy. Keep your windup simple and put all your energy into the pitch.

There are pitchers who slap their thigh with their glove hand upon release of the ball, exposing their body to possible serious injury if a line drive comes back at them. A better position for their glove hand would be holding it in front of their body, chest high, to stop the ball from hitting them.

Don't be afraid to imitate. Just remember to evaluate and ask yourself if what you are trying would cause injury to you or if it would change the mechanics.

5) ***Attend various clinics***. A lot of colleges and universities conduct softball clinics during the summer months. Ask around and find out which clinics are worth the time. You can pick up a few good ideas to help improve your game.
6) ***Throw things***. As you will see in Chapter 12, you don't always have to throw a softball to practice. Make it fun! Just remember to never throw things at people, animals, or windows.

Common Problems

1) ***Your grip***. Make sure you begin each pitch using the correct grip. It is easier to make a ball spin using the seams than having your fingers off of the seams.
2) ***Lack of wrist snap***. If your wrist is weak, it will not produce the snap you need for speed. Practice your wrist snap drills.
3) ***Reaching the ball to the catcher***. If your body is leaning forward your balance will be off, which means your release point will be changed. The release point will be out in front of your body and you won't be throwing the ball with any velocity. You will need to work on your balance drills to correct this problem.

Tips and Tricks for Beginners

4) ***Arm not relaxed***. A tense arm will produce less speed. Work on your arm circles using the suggested ways of relaxation.
5) ***Release point***. Your body position plays a role in where you release the ball but so does the lack of muscle memory. You need to constantly train your muscles to remember the correct release point. Use your wrist snap drills to work on this.
6) ***Lack of concentration***. It is difficult sometimes to concentrate on what you're doing if you're thinking about your friends, or if there are a lot of people around. You need to stay focused on what you are doing. Try to find a time to practice when you won't be distracted by other things.
7) ***Stride length***. Remember that pitching is "walking" towards your catcher. If your stride length is too long, it will take you out of balance. As your mechanics become consistent, you will begin to increase your stride length for more power. A beginner should focus on walking and getting her whole body in sequence.
8) ***Glove placement***. The use of your glove hand is vital to your well being. Your glove is the only thing that will protect you from possible "missiles" coming back at you. A lot of pitchers are taught to end their pitch with their glove hands at their side in order to help rotate their hips. Unfortunately, doing this leaves your face and body completely open. You may not have the reflexes to get your glove hand in position to stop a ball coming back at you. Bringing your glove hand forcefully back to your shoulder will produce the same hip turn. Your glove hand should always come back towards your shoulder with the glove open and ready to catch the ball. This will give you time to either make the catch, or at least deflect the ball to avoid serious injury.
9) ***You will only be as good as you want to be***. This statement brings you back to whether you want to be a "thrower" or a "pitcher." If you are seriously considering a pitching career, you can't rely on your natural abilities. You need to develop your natural abilities with lots of practice and hard work.

CHAPTER 12
Let's Have Some Fun!

ho says practice needs to be boring? There are ways to make practicing fun while focusing on specific areas of the pitch. Here are some fun activities, some that don't even need a softball, to help you get started.

1) Bag of softballs

Using two ordinary plastic grocery store bags put one bag inside the other to make the bag stronger. Put three or four softballs in the bag and tie a knot with the handles of the bag to prevent the balls from falling out. Stand in your power position on your power line and swing the bag using your full arm circle. Notice how the weight of the softballs stretches out your arm. This is how your arm should feel throughout your arm circle.

Once you are used to the feel of the pull of the bag, try throwing the bag to your catcher or to a wall while finding your release point. The bag will pull your arm into your follow-through, not allowing you to lock your elbow.

2) Bucket of water

This drill uses the same principle as the bag of softballs producing the feeling of your arm being stretched out through your arm circle and preventing your elbow from locking.

Use a bucket with a metal handle. The bucket can be any size. Fill it halfway with water (if you use a large bucket only fill about ¼ of the bucket). Stand in your power position on your power line and swing the bucket through your arm circle. You need to keep the speed of your arm circle constant and quick so the water doesn't spill out. A slow arm circle will result in you getting wet!

Diamond Girl

3) Hockey pucks

Believe it or not, you can use a hockey puck to practice your wrist snap! Hold the hockey puck horizontally using only your finger tips. The hockey puck should not be resting on the palm of your hand. Try flipping it into the air making the puck turn end-over-end. You should feel the puck roll off your fingertips. If it is not spinning, roll it off your fingers onto the floor until you get the correct spin.

Once you have mastered flipping the hockey puck from the horizontal position, change the position of the hockey puck so that it is resting on your second and third fingers vertical to the floor. Toss the hockey puck into the air, letting it roll off your fingers without producing a wiggle. It should resemble a rotating car tire.

Don't forget to use correct wrist snap. You should see your "smiley face" on the palm of your hand.

4) Tube socks

The use of tube socks is a great way to check your pitching mechanics when nobody is around. You will need a mirror and a pair of tube socks rolled up into a ball. Stand in front of a mirror and using your full pitching motion pitch the tube socks into the mirror. Don't watch the socks, but instead, watch your body as it goes through the pitching motion. You can see if you are using a wrist snap and relaxed follow-through and not locking your elbow.

5) Potato Chips

Did you ever try to pitch a potato chip? It sounds crazy but throwing a potato chip will show how tightly you hold the ball.

Hold the potato chip as you would a softball – in your fingertips with your thumb on the bottom and fingers on top of the chip. Use your full arm circle and throw the potato chip releasing at your release point. Since the potato chip is very light, it will flutter only a few feet in front of you. If the potato chip breaks in your fingers while going through your arm circle, it means you are holding the softball too tightly, which will reduce the speed of the pitch.

Practice the potato chip drill at the end of a practice so that you don't have potato chip grease on your fingers while throwing your softball – the ball will slip.

6) Ball on a Cone

Place a softball on a cone such as a cone you would use in gym class. See how many times you can knock the ball off the cone without hitting the cone. This helps you to practice your concentration.

7) P-I-G or H-O-R-S-E

Another way to work on your concentration is by playing a game of "Pig" or "Horse" with another pitching friend. You also need someone to catch and to serve as the "judge."

One pitcher starts the game by announcing to the catcher, or judge, the location of where she wants to throw the pitch such as "low and inside to a right-handed batter." The judge will determine if she has succeeded in hitting her target. If she has, the second pitcher must hit the exact location. If the second pitcher misses, she acquires a letter. If the second pitcher hits the location, the first pitcher will again announce the location of her next pitch and must hit it. If the first pitcher misses on her try, the second pitcher becomes the starter of the next round announcing where she's going to try to throw the ball. If the second pitcher hits her called location, the first pitcher must now hit that spot. The game continues until someone loses by completing the designated word, either "pig" or "horse."

8) Dodge ball

Dodge ball is normally played using a circle of people who try to hit the players inside the circle with a rubber ball, eliminating them from the game. The players in the circle try not to get hit and to be the last person left in the circle. This game is played with a different twist to it and is a great way to practice the wrist snap. You need a group of pitchers for this game. Rolled-up tube socks are used for the balls in this game.

Divide the pitchers into two groups – one group creates the outside circle while the second one is the "targets" in the middle of the circle. Just like in the regular game of dodge ball, the people on the outside want to eliminate the people inside the circle by hitting them with the tube sock ball. More than one tube sock ball may be used to make the game more interesting. The big difference is that the pitchers on the outside of the circle must throw the ball *underhand only*! They don't use their full arm circle as that would take too long. As soon as they get the ball, they throw the ball using only their ¼ frame from the framing drill using a lot of wrist snap. Pitchers throwing without a wrist snap will throw the socks much slower and their body position will no doubt be leaning forward.

Once all girls in the center of the circle are hit (or after a certain time period) the two groups exchange position and the game continues.

Mixing Things Up with Some Special Equipment

Multi-colored softballs

Various sporting goods stores sell multi-colored softballs. Just using something with a different color seems to add a little spice to things. Multi-colored softballs also help to make the pitchers aware of the rotation of the ball.

Swimming pool rings

Small plastic rings of six to eight inches in diameter can be found at stores that sell swimming pool supplies. You may even find these at a dollar store. These can be used to practice your wrist snaps.

Starting from a squatting position, rest your forearm of your pitching hand on your knee. Your hand should hang over the edge of your knee. Hold the ring gently in your hand and flip the ring up so that it hits your forearm and your wrist finishes in a bent position.

Diamond Girl

Water balloons

Water balloons are ideal for practicing the change-up since you do not want to use a wrist snap because wrist snap creates speed. Your wrist should be straight as you toss the balloon.

Stand in your power position and practice pitching the water balloon to a catcher using the ¼ framing drill mentioned in Chapter 3. Throw it gently so the balloon doesn't break.

Bean bag

If you cannot use water balloons to practice the change-up, don't hesitate to use a bean bag!

Weighted balls

Weighted balls are used to work on building strength and stamina. Advanced pitchers will also use them to work on various pitch spins. Weighted balls can be found at your local sporting goods store and usually come in a pack of three different weighted balls. Weighted balls should **never** be thrown at full speed.

To build strength, you will need to "overload" and "underload" your muscles in your pitching arm. To do so, begin by throwing five pitches using the normal weight softball. Follow this by throwing ten pitches using the heaviest ball ("overloading"), and then ten pitches using the lightest ball ("underloading"). Your muscles will have to adjust to the weights. It will take a few pitches to find your release point when you throw the lightest ball as it will feel like you are throwing a feather! Finish the drill by throwing ten pitches with your regular softball.

CHAPTER 13
Advanced Pitching: Adding Movement Pitches

Congratulations on mastering the basic fundamentals of pitching! You have found out that pitching is not easy. If it was, everybody would do it! You have also learned that it takes a great deal of patience and hard work to train your muscles to remember what to do, when to do it, and where to release the ball. The more pitching time you get, whether practicing at home or pitching a few innings in a game, the better you will become as long as you stay focused on your mechanics. If you make a bad pitch, forget it and move on to the next one. Try to figure out what went wrong with your mechanics and make the necessary correction with your next pitch.

You should have good control of the strike zone at this point, but as you get older, stronger, and wiser with softball sense, so will your opposing batters. A fastball pitched on an outside corner may now end up as a triple instead of a strikeout because the batter figured out how to properly hit outside pitches. You now need to start adding movement to your pitches in order to fool the batter.

Practice is vital in mastering the movement pitches since drills lead to skill and confidence, putting *you* in charge of the game, not the batter. Location and movement of your pitches will keep batters off-balance.

The basic pitches an advanced pitcher needs are the fastball, the change up, the drop ball pitch, and the rise ball pitch. All of these pitches have deviations depending on, for instance, how the ball comes off your fingertips. Pitchers may also add optional pitches such as the curve ball and screwball. Depending on the release point and turn of the wrist, the curve ball may also drop. The screwball may rise like a rise ball but will also break towards a right-handed batter because of the way you stride and release the ball.

Diamond Girl

You also need to factor in safety issues when adding movement pitches. Your body is still developing and you don't want to damage any growth plates. The more stress and torque you use on your pitching arm the more chances you have of injury. For instance, hold your arm out in front of you, shoulder height, with your hand straight out and parallel to the ground. Turn your hand so that your thumb is pointing towards the ground with your hand turning slightly past the point of being sideways. You can feel the tension of your muscles going into your shoulders.

For safety reasons alone, as an advanced pitcher you need to be completely committed to pitching. That means devoting more time to preseason conditioning and practicing. You also need to prepare well in advance of any other player on your team. You are usually the first player at the practice field going through your stretching routine. You are typically the last person to leave in order to practice your defensive skills to improve your reflexes. You know that your teammates and coaches are relying on you to be a leader of the team. You *want* to be a vital part of the game, being in control of the game.

As you begin practicing the movement pitches, keep in mind that progression of development is much smaller for advanced pitching since you are fine-tuning your release point and body position.

Are you ready to make this commitment?

REVIEW OF THE FASTBALL

There are two grips for the fastball: the four-seam grip with fingers holding the ball across the seams, and the two-seam grip where the fingers are holding the ball in the same direction of the seams (see Figs. 2.2.a and 2.2.b in Chapter 2). Advanced pitchers will use both depending on the outcome of the pitch they wish to achieve. The four-seam grip is used for the straight fastball. It is also used as the grip for the slip-drop pitch. The two-seam grip will produce more movement on the ball by the release of finger pressure on the seams. The addition of good movement pitches will make your fastball seem even faster.

The key elements to producing a good fastball are a hard wrist snap that is achieved by holding the ball in your fingertips (your wrist is less tense this way), a strong push-off from the pitching rubber, and fast arm speed by using a smooth *relaxed* windup. Your stride will be long and aggressive with your power leg (pivot foot) following through. Your pitching shoulder will be slightly behind your release point as your arm leads your hip.

Remember to exhale as you release the ball. Weightlifters grunt and exhale while lifting heavy weights, putting all their power into the lift. You don't need to grunt but you want to exhale, transferring all your power to your pitch. Use your breath to "blow" the ball to your catcher. Proper breathing will also help to relax your body and you will find yourself throwing harder with little effort.

An important key to throwing a fastball is to learn to relax. Tense muscles reduce speed while relaxed muscles generate speed. The more relaxed you keep your pitching arm throughout the arm circle, the faster you will throw the ball.

Advanced Pitching: Adding Movement Pitches

Relaxation Drills

Keeping your body relaxed and loose is necessary when trying to increase the speed of your pitch. Learning how to relax can be difficult, but there are ways to practice.

The Humming Drill was introduced in Chapter 10. The following drills will also help improve your relaxation technique.

(1) Robot Drill

When your arms and legs are tense, you move like a robot. Your whole body is tight and your movements are jerky. When you relax, your arms and legs move fluidly.

Start this drill by standing three feet behind the pitching rubber with the softball in your pitching hand. Pretend you are a robot - tightening up your arms, legs, and body - and shuffle around the pitching rubber in a circle, staying three feet from the pitching rubber. Once you reach your starting position (behind the pitching rubber), relax your entire body. Then step onto the pitching rubber and pitch the ball. Try to remember how your body felt after doing this drill – nice and relaxed!

(2) Rag Doll Drill

Hold a rag doll in your hands. She's quite limp and relaxed. You can move her arms and legs easily. In this drill you become the rag doll.

With your glove on and the softball in your pitching hand, bend forward from your waist so that your head is down and your arms are dangling. Let your arms swing from side to side keeping them limp. After a few seconds, bring your hands together, come up with your body and pitch the ball, trying to keep your arms as limp as they were when you were mimicking the rag doll.

(3) 3-Ball Drill

Picture a juggler with three balls. He starts out slow and then picks up the pace of his tosses. In this drill the only difference between you and the juggler is that the juggler is tossing the ball vertically in the air while you are tossing the softball horizontally to your catcher.

This drill works on getting your whole body into a fluid, relaxed motion. Staying relaxed will help to increase velocity.

Begin this drill by holding two softballs – one ball in your glove and the other in your pitching hand. Your catcher is holding one softball in his/her throwing hand. Pitch the ball in your pitching hand to your catcher. Transfer the ball from your glove hand to your pitching hand. Your catcher will throw his/her softball to you. As you can see, before throwing your next pitch you will always begin with two softballs in your possession at all times.

Continue this drill staying relaxed, not rushing between pitches, and getting into a rhythm with your entire body. Once you are comfortable with the concept, start decreasing the time between pitches until you reach the point where you are able to pitch the ball almost immediately after catching the ball from your catcher.

Diamond Girl

By practicing these relaxation drills you may notice that your velocity is beginning to increase. These drills worked on relaxing your arm and getting your body into a rhythm. By adding the power generated by your legs and hips you will continue to increase your velocity.

Drills to Increase Velocity

Velocity is achieved by literally cutting yourself in half with your upper body (arms) being loose and relaxed while your lower body (hips and legs) are forceful and driving. Velocity drills should be done at the end of practices to help build both velocity and stamina.

(1) Distance Pitching

Start this drill by pitching two pitches from the pitcher's mound. Move back two steps and throw another two pitches. Repeat this process until you begin to bounce the ball to the catcher or until you reach second base. (You don't want to overdo it the first few times. Add a few more backward steps each time you practice until you build up to the point where you are bouncing the ball.) The farther back you move the more you need to use strong leg drive.

Once you are finished moving as far back as you can, step back onto the pitcher's mound and throw ten fastballs in a row to your catcher. Pitching from the pitcher's mound will now seem easy!

(2) 3-Circle Drill

This drill helps to relax your arm and to drive with your legs. You can also use this drill to work on your reflexes catching a ball coming back at you.

Holding the softball in your pitching hand, stand in your power position on your power line approximately 15-20 feet in front of either a wall or a net. Make three quick arm circles using your pitching motion. The first two circles will get your arm loose and relaxed. On the third circle, throw the ball into the wall or net using as much hip turn and leg drive as possible. Your hips should end square to the wall or net. If you are throwing at a wall, you should end in a defensive stance with your glove hand near your shoulder ready to catch the ball as it comes off the wall.

(3) Rapid Fire Drill

The Rapid Fire Drill mentioned in Chapter 10 is one of the best drills for learning to relax your pitching arm AND to increase velocity by using hard leg drive.

Focus specifically on your push-off leg while practicing this drill. The large muscles of your legs are extremely powerful. Use these muscles to push extremely hard off the pitching rubber. By doing so, your body will "explode" towards your catcher. Your push-off leg will be extremely tired by the end of the third set.

THE CHANGE UP

If you only throw fastballs, the advanced batter will eventually adjust to the timing of your pitch and you will become a "human pitching machine." Advanced batters don't care what kind of windup you use

Advanced Pitching: Adding Movement Pitches

since they don't follow your arm through its arm circle. Advanced batters focus only on one location - your release point - just like they would focus on the shoot of a pitching machine where the ball is projected.

In order to counteract the batter's abilities, you need to outwit her by throwing off-speed pitches or some other type of movement pitches causing the batter to reach for a ball or prematurely swing at it. In other words, you need to get the batter off balance. One such pitch is the change-up.

The change-up pitch is thrown with no wrist snap, unlike the fastball, the rise pitch, and the drop pitch. Eliminating the wrist snap will float the ball to the catcher causing the batter to swing prematurely.

The change-up pitch needs to resemble a fastball by using a quick arm circle. You also need to shorten your stride to help reduce the speed of your pitch. Your pitching hand should stop abruptly at your release point as if it were going to hit a wall in front of you. Your body should be in an upright position. Your shoulders should not be leaning forward. Your release of the ball should feel as if you were "pushing" the ball to the catcher.

There are numerous ways to grip the ball when throwing the change-up. You need to experiment to find out which grip(s) work for you. Keep in mind, though, that it is better to have consistency with one or two variations of the change-up grip than to have five or six different grips which produce sporadic results.

Here are just a few examples of grips commonly used by pitchers today.

1) <u>The Palm Ball</u>

The softball is tucked deep into your palm creating a "seal" between your hand and the ball, and held tightly.

Fig. 13.1.a Palm ball grip.

Diamond Girl

2) <u>The Knuckle Ball</u>

The softball is held tightly by pressing the first knuckles of your index, middle, and ring fingers into the ball while your pinky and thumb grip the ball. If your hand is not big enough to hold it this way, you can also dig your fingernails into the seams of the softball.

Fig. 13.1.b Knuckle ball grip.

3) <u>The Circle Change</u>

Your thumb and index finger meet to create a "circle." Grip the softball, tucking the softball deep in your palm with the circle on the side of the ball.

Fig. 13.1.c Circle change grip.

Experiment with grips by holding the ball with the seams, without holding the seams, and changing your finger locations. There are no rules on how to grip the ball for the change-up.

Drills to Practice the Change-Up Pitch

The key to pitching a good change-up is to eliminate the wrist snap and feel the ball being "pushed" to your catcher. Here are two drills which will help develop the change-up.

Advanced Pitching: Adding Movement Pitches

1) <u>Palm Drill</u>

Draw a "smiley face" on the palm of your pitching hand. Hold the softball in your pitching hand while facing your catcher, standing about four feet in front of her. Make sure the softball is tucked deep into your palm. Without using a wrist snap, push the softball out to your catcher. Your fingers will spread as you release the ball, showing the smiley face to your catcher.

Fig. 13.2 The change-up is thrown without using a wrist snap.

Once you get comfortable at this distance, increase the distance by two steps, repeating this process until you get about 15 feet apart. At this point stand on your power line in your power position while doing this same drill. Remember that when you are in your power position, you will now need to turn your hips.

Move to the pitcher's mound and onto the pitcher's rubber. Using a full quick arm circle and taking a small stride, stop your arm at your release point and push the ball to your catcher. Continue your follow-through, using a little flip of your hand to *imitate* a wrist snap. This will help disguise your change-up by making it appear like you are throwing a fastball.

Diamond Girl

2) Water Balloon Drill

If you are still having problems with the concept of pushing the ball, you can practice with a water balloon. You will not be throwing the water balloon with your full motion nor from the pitcher's mound. This drill is only to improve your feel of pushing the ball.

Hold the water balloon in your pitching hand starting out at a close distance to your catcher while standing in your power position on the power line. Gently push the water balloon to your catcher. If you throw the water balloon too fast, the balloon will break.

After a few throws, move back a few steps. Focus on what your hand is doing throughout this drill.

3) Bean Bag Drill

This drill continues to work on the concept of pushing the ball. You can either play a game of bean bag tossing the bag into the hole on the board or just toss a bean bag to your catcher. Notice that you don't use a wrist snap when tossing the bag.

4) Change-up Barrier Drill

The change-up pitch requires a short stride in order to take speed off the pitch. If you find yourself taking too long of a stride, this drill will help to shorten it. You can use your softball bag, a chair, or even a person – anything that can be used as a barrier – for this drill. Your stride length should be about half the length of your fastball stride length.

Place a mark at the location of your stride length for your fastball. Now place your barrier half way. If you are using another person as the barrier, she should stand slightly to the side so that you won't hit her with your pitching hand. Practice pitching your change-ups with your stride length stopping at your barrier.

Fig. 13.3.a The coach acts as a barrier to prevent a long stride.

Fig. 13.3.b By taking a short stride, your left foot lands between the coach's feet.

Advanced Pitching: Adding Movement Pitches

Fig. 13.3.c You will stand near the coach upon finishing your pitch.

THE DROP PITCH

Your opponent has one out with runners on base. You don't want those runners to score by a ball hit to the outfield. Your team needs to get an out somewhere in the infield. A drop pitch is perfect in this situation since the softball is thrown using a downward spin forcing the ball to drop at the front of home plate. Batters will either miss the pitch by swinging overtop of the ball, or hitting only the top portion of the ball causing the ball to be driven into the ground to one of your infielders.

There are three locations where you want the ball to drop. The first is a drop pitch that hits the dirt about six inches in front of the plate. This location is used for batters positioned in the front of the batter's box. The second is one that breaks at the very front of the plate and is used most often. Both of these pitches get the batter to reach for the ball. The third location is a drop pitch that is actually thrown for a strike on either the inside or outside corners.

Pitchers use two types of drop pitches. The first is the slip drop, also known as the peel drop, where you let the ball slip, or peel, off your fingertips. The second is the turnover or snap-over drop, where you actually turn your hand over the ball to force it downward.

Diamond Girl

The Slip Drop, or Peel Drop

The grip for the slip drop is held across the seams exactly like the four-seam fastball. Resting your fingertips on the seam is vital as your fingers need to pull on the seam to create the downward spin. When you release the ball, it will feel like it is slipping off your fingers.

Your stride needs to be short in order to position your shoulders over your stride foot. Your weight shifts onto your stride foot creating a body position that looks similar to a ski jumper coming down the hill but not quite as dramatic.

Your body position will cause your release point to change. In order for the ball to slip off your fingers, your release point will be slightly *behind* your pivot leg. Your fingers pull upward and backward on the seam finishing with your wrist snap closer to your body. The more pull you can put on the ball, the more drop you will get on your pitch. How fast you throw the drop determines how drastic the movement will be. Throwing the drop pitch as an off-speed pitch will create more spin and a sharper downward movement because you put more pull on the seam.

If the ball is not dropping, check your release point and also make sure your pivot foot stays on the pitching rubber a little longer.

Drills

1) Roll the Can

This drill is done from a kneeling position in order to focus on the feel of the can rolling off your fingers. You will need any type of can that contains a solid mass such as a can of pumpkin or a can of cream of chicken soup.

Begin with both knees on the power line in your power position. Lay the can horizontally on the floor slightly behind your back leg. Rest your hand on the top of the can, keeping your thumb off the can. Slowly roll the can with your fingertips to your catcher who is positioned about five feet in front of you. Feel the can roll off your fingertips. Finish with your gentle wrist snap.

Now do the same drill using a softball. If done properly, the softball will roll down the power line to your catcher.

2) Standing Slip Drop

When throwing the drop pitch from a standing position, you need to constantly think "low." You need to visualize the path of the downward movement and focus on how the ball is being released. Your shoulder position is key and needs to be slightly forward so that your release point is slightly behind your pivot leg.

Start this drill by standing about ten feet in front of home plate. Or, you can use another object such as a glove or towel as your target on the floor. Your catcher will stand about five feet behind home plate.

Advanced Pitching: Adding Movement Pitches

Hold the softball using your four-seam grip and stand square to home plate. Do not move your feet in this drill and do not use your full arm circle. Toss the ball so that it hits home plate. You should be able to see the four seams spinning in a downward rotation. Feel the ball roll off your fingertips.

Once you produce the correct spin and feel at this distance, increase the distance by three feet until you reach the point where you are throwing from ¾ distance between the pitcher's rubber and home plate. Move into your power position on the power line and continue to do this drill, still focusing on your shoulder position, release point, and spin on the ball.

Move onto the pitching mound and continue throwing to your target on the floor using your full arm motion.

Review the mechanics of the drop pitch in your mind before throwing it – short stride, weight shifts to your front foot, shoulders lean slightly forward. Your release point is slightly behind your pivot leg, and the ball slips off your fingertips producing the downward spin.

3) Kneeling Slip Drop

Kneel with both knees at a 45-degree angle on the power line in your power position approximately 30 feet from your target on the ground. Throw the ball using your full windup and using your drop pitch mechanics allowing the ball to slip off your fingertips. Your shoulders will automatically lean slightly forward since you are focusing on a low target. Your release point will be slightly behind your pitching hand leg. The path of the ball should be out towards the target, not up like a rainbow, with the ball dropping on or near the target.

Fig. 13.4.a Both knees are on the power line in your power position.

Fig. 13.4.b Your body leans slightly forward, and your release point is slightly behind your right leg.

Diamond Girl

Fig. 13.4.c Your fingers pull upward and backward on the seam. Finish with your arm close to your body.

4) A Drop in the Bucket!

This is a fun and challenging drill to do once you have the feel and some control of the slip drop. You will need some sort of bucket or basket that is approximately 12 inches high.

Set the bucket on top of home plate with some type of support such as your softball bag or ball bag behind the bucket so it doesn't tip over. Throw from your normal distance from the pitcher's mound using your proper slip drop mechanics and try to get the ball to drop directly into the bucket. Don't get frustrated if you have problems doing this drill. It takes a lot of focus and good mechanics. You will eventually be able to get the ball in the bucket.

The Turnover Drop

The turnover drop is the hardest on the arm since you are adding torque. The turnover drop begins at the wrist with your wrist snapping downward. You can feel the stress of the turn move up your arm from your wrist, into your elbow, and then into your shoulder. Pitchers throwing the turnover drop also have a tendency to pull their arm and elbow away from their body which adds more stress to the shoulder.

Advanced Pitching: Adding Movement Pitches

Learn how to throw the slip drop before moving on to the turnover drop. If you can throw a great slip drop pitch you may want to just stick with that drop pitch.

The turnover drop is a more challenging pitch because if it is done incorrectly, it could cause arm injury over time. You need to use the two-seam grip for this pitch. When throwing this pitch you need to feel your wrist and fingers actually come up and over the ball at release point in order to create the downward spin. Your mechanics for the turnover drop is the same as the slip drop except at release point where you turn your wrist over the ball.

Practice the turnover drop drills and, once you feel comfortable with the release point, move to your standing power position on your power line about 25 feet away from home plate. Practice throwing the softball using your full arm circle and using your turnover drop so that it hits the plate. Pay particular attention to what your elbow is doing. It should stay next to your body and not fly out.

Move to the pitcher's rubber and try to hit home plate. Your catcher can also hold her glove hand on home plate as a visual aid. Try to make the ball drop into her glove.

You can use the bucket drill to practice the turnover drop as well as the following drills.

1) Home Plate Drop

Start this drill from a kneeling position in your power position on your power line directly next to home plate. You can use the edge of home plate as your power line. Hold the ball in your pitching hand at your release point keeping your arm straight and next to your body. Turn your wrist bringing your hand up and around the softball, dropping the ball onto home plate.

Now try this drill from a standing position, standing directly next to home plate. Again, you want to only move your wrist bringing your hand up and around the softball to drop the ball onto home plate.

2) Basketball Drop

If you are still having problems with getting the feel of bringing your hand up and around a softball, switch to using a basketball. Sitting for this drill will help to keep your hand near your release point.

Sit in an armless chair and hold a basketball in the palm of your pitching hand. Bend your elbow so that it touches the chair and your forearm is parallel to the floor. Your elbow must stay in contact with the chair at all times so that you only turn your hand at your wrist. Turn your hand over quickly so that the basketball falls to the floor. Your palm will now be facing the floor. After practicing with a basketball, this drill should seem quite easy when you switch back to a softball.

THE RISE BALL

The rise ball, or "riser," is another great movement pitch and is the most difficult pitch to learn. If you have problems with this pitch, a high fastball can be substituted. The riser is used to create a pop-up to an infielder or a fly ball to an outfielder. Due to the upward angle and backward spin in which the ball is pitched the batter tends to hit the bottom third of the ball.

Diamond Girl

For example, the other team has a lead-off runner on first base. The next batter's main objective is to move the runner into scoring position by possibly bunting. You need to throw a pitch that will force the batter to reach for the ball. The riser is a great pitch to throw in this situation since the batter has to raise her bat to catch up with the rise of the ball. In most incidences, the batter will hit a pop-up to the catcher.

The rise ball is produced by using a backward spin. The two-seam fastball grip is used, but with the index and middle fingers resting together. The middle finger rests on the seam. Some pitchers prefer to dig their index finger into the ball while others just release the pressure off the index finger. The thumb rests on the bottom seam of the "C" on the ball.

Fig. 13.5 Rise ball grip.

The release of the ball should feel as if you are turning a doorknob directly at your side. The upward motion is produced by the back of your elbow moving past your side where your fingers cut underneath the ball. A good strong wrist snap is required to make the riser work. If your riser begins to rise but flattens out, you didn't use enough wrist snap.

Your stride should be long and aggressive. Since you want to start the riser from a lower position, your right knee should bend slightly lowering your body. Your release point will be at the height of your knee. Your push-off from the pitching rubber needs to be strong and hard in order to snap up with your body while forcing your shoulders to move slightly backward upon release of the ball.

The follow-through of your pitching arm is quick. Your pitching hand ends with your fingers cupped towards and close to your chest while your thumb sticks out like you are hitch-hiking.

Advanced Pitching: Adding Movement Pitches

Here are a few drills to help develop your rise ball. Again, this is the most difficult pitch to master so it may take time. Be patient!

1) Spill the Water

This drill helps you get the feel of how your hand should turn. All you need is a glass of water and your kitchen sink.

Stand in front of the sink holding a glass of water in your pitching hand. Turn only your hand and not your elbow clockwise, letting the water spill out of the side of the glass. (Note: right-handed pitchers turn their hand clockwise, while left-handed pitchers turn their hand counter-clockwise.) The palm of your hand faces upward. Don't over-rotate your hand as this will put a lot of stress on your elbow and shoulder.

2) Tip the Teacup

Practice this drill from your power position on your power line. This drill will again stress the feeling of the ball rolling out of the side of your hand.

Hold the softball in your pitching hand with your elbow resting on your side and your forearm parallel to the ground. Your palm is facing upward holding the ball. With a slight clockwise turn of your pitching hand, let the ball roll out of your hand onto the floor. Your shoulder will move slightly backwards as your hand turns.

Fig. 13.6.a Hold the softball using the riser grip with your palm facing up.

Fig. 13.6.b Turn your hand clockwise and let the ball roll out of your hand.

Diamond Girl

3) Pull Out the Tablecloth

You've watched people perform the trick of pulling a tablecloth from underneath dishes and glasses. The same principle works with this drill only your hand represents the tablecloth and the softball represents a dish. By using a quick arm motion you will produce a backward spin as the ball falls directly to the ground.

Stand in your power position on your power line. The softball rests in your pitching hand with your elbow resting on your side and your forearm parallel to the ground. With a quick, sharp motion, cut underneath the ball "pulling out the tablecloth." Your hand ends with your fingers cupped towards and close to your chest while your thumb sticks out like you are hitch-hiking.

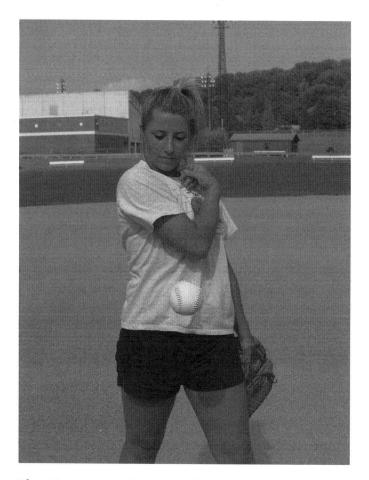

Fig. 13.7 Cut underneath the ball, creating a backward spin and finishing as if "hitch-hiking."

4) Rocker Rise-Ball Drill

The Rocker Drill used in Chapter 6 is also used to practice the rise ball. The only difference is the finish position of your pitching hand. In this drill, your pitching hand ends with your fingers cupped towards and close to your chest while your thumb sticks out like you are hitch-hiking.

Advanced Pitching: Adding Movement Pitches

Start by kneeling on the power line in your power position with your stride leg extended and bent at the knee so that you are in a balanced position. Practice rocking forward and back to get the feel of using your stride leg to push your body back.

Now add your arm circle by using three steps: 1) your pitching hand and glove hand are in the starting position with your arms straight. 2) Begin the rocker motion, moving forward as your pitching hand extends to where it is slightly above and in front of your head. Your glove hand comes up as you begin your arm circle and you actually rest your glove hand arm on your left thigh as your body rocks forward. 3) Your pitching arm now begins its downswing and your glove hand extends towards your catcher. As your pitching hand comes down, your stride foot pushes your body back into a position where your shoulders are now slightly back. Your elbow stays close to your side as your pitching hand cuts underneath the ball and finishes with your hitch-hiking position.

Do this drill in slow motion until you get the feel of it while counting "1" (starting position), "2" (body rocks forward), and "3" (body pushed back with stride leg while snapping the ball). Build up to a fluid motion with good wrist snap and a nice rise on the ball.

5) Roof Drill

This drill helps you work on the spin of the ball by having you throw into your own glove. Focus on throwing into your own glove first. Then go into the second idea of also practicing with a catcher.

Stand in your power position on the power line. Hold your glove out in front of your body above your head with the palm of your glove facing the floor creating a "roof." Start your pitching hand at the release point for your riser (at your side) and snap the ball into your glove (see Figs. 13.8.a, 13.8.b).

You can also practice this with a catcher by having your catcher stand approximately 30 feet in front of you with her glove held facing the floor at shoulder height. Start from your pitching position on the pitching rubber and, using your full motion with the rise ball mechanics, snap the ball into the catcher's glove.

6) Flamingo Drill

This drill promotes the feel of the rocker motion with your upper body. Since it is done by standing only on your pivot foot, you'll need good balance for this drill.

Stand on one foot – your pivot foot – in your power position on your power line while wrapping your stride foot around the back of your pivot leg knee. Get your balance and try just rocking slightly forward and back with your upper body. Once you get the feel of this, try actually throwing the rise ball to your catcher who is approximately 30 feet in front of you using the rise ball mechanics. It's not easy! (See Figs. 13.9.a, 13.9.b)

Fig. 13.8.a Hold your glove high and facing the ground.

Fig. 13.8.b Throw the ball into your glove using the rise ball mechanics.

Fig. 13.9.a Balance on your pivot foot with your left foot resting behind your right knee.

Fig. 13.9.b Stay balanced and throw the ball, pushing your shoulder back as in the Rocker Rise-ball drill (drill #4 mentioned above).

Advanced Pitching: Adding Movement Pitches

Practice Sequence for the Fastball, Change, Riser, Drop

Once you have mastered the movement pitches, start practicing as if you were in a game situation. Practice throwing "opposite" pitches. For instance, throw a fast ball which requires a long stride and wrist snap. Then throw a change-up which requires a short stride and no wrist snap. Do the same with the riser and the drop pitch. The riser requires a long stride and shoulders slightly back on release while the drop pitch requires a shorter stride with your shoulders slightly forward. This is how you would mix up your pitches during a game.

THE CURVE BALL

The curve ball is another pitch which is used to either break completely out of or into the strike zone. The curve ball can be thrown starting in the middle of the plate causing it to break away from a right-handed hitter. Or, it can be thrown inside to a right-handed batter where the pitch appears to be off the plate but breaks back towards the corner of the plate. Unlike the other movement pitches, this pitch travels horizontally on the same plane. If the break of the ball is not working, it will be easier for a batter to hit this pitch.

The grip is similar to the rise ball with your middle and index fingers resting along the seam and your thumb on a seam. Some pitchers prefer to tuck their index finger. Experiment with the grip to find what will produce the maximum four-seam horizontal spin. Your palm will always be facing the sky.

Your stride and hip turn play a key role in making the curve ball work. Your stride is shorter than your fast ball. Your first step will be slightly *across* your power line, stepping towards the location where you wish to begin the pitch. For example, if you want the curve ball to break away from the middle of the plate to the outside corner, your first step will be towards the middle of the plate.

At this point your pitching hand will lead your hip. Your pitching arm stays close to your body as your pitching hand comes across your body pulling your hip through. Your thumb will release from the ball as your hip twists at release. Your follow-through brings your pitching hand towards your belly button. The twisting motion of your hip will force the ball out of the strike zone.

When you begin to practice the curve ball, work on getting the feel of the spin of the ball first – your palm faces the sky, your fingers and thumb resting on seams, and your pitching hand finishing at your belly button. Once you have the feel and can see the four-seam rotation, add your legs stepping across your power line and forcing your hip to twist as you release the ball.

Here are a few drills for the curve ball.

Diamond Girl

 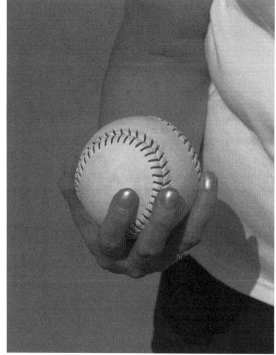

Fig. 13.10.a Curve ball grip.   **Fig. 13.10.b** Another curve ball grip.

1) <u>Curve Ball Self Pitch</u>

This drill works on the hip turn and wrist snap needed to throw the curve ball.

Stand with your pivot foot on the power line with your stride leg just across the power line. Your glove hand will be positioned on the power line slightly in front and to the left of the knee of your stride leg. Swing your pitching arm back and then forward. Rotate your hip and spin the softball using the curve ball rotation into your glove with the follow-through of your pitching hand finishing towards your belly button (see Figs. 13.11.a, 13.11.b).

2) <u>Standing Curve</u>

You will use the same mechanics as you did in the "Curve Ball Self Pitch" drill except you will now be throwing to a catcher who stands about 10 feet away. You are practicing the spin working the mechanics and shouldn't be throwing hard. Your stance is the same as in the "Curve Ball Self Pitch" drill. Throw to your catcher remembering to keep your pitching hand facing the sky and to rotate your hips.

When you have mastered the feel of the spin, increase the distance between you and your catcher and throw the pitch using your full arm circle from your normal pitching stance (see Figs. 13.12.a, 13.12.b).

3) <u>Around the Cone</u>

Place a cone about six feet in front of home place. Your stride will be across the power line to the throwing side of the cone where you want the ball to start. Using your hip rotation try to make the ball curve around the cone to your catcher's glove on the other side of the cone.

Advanced Pitching: Adding Movement Pitches

Fig. 13.11.a Start with your left foot across the power line (pitching hand side).

Fig. 13.11.b Use ¼ frame starting position. Pitch the ball into your glove, moving your hand across your body, turning your hip, and finishing with your hand pointing toward your belly button.

Fig. 13.12.a Stand in your power position with your left foot slightly across the power line.

Fig. 13.12.b Pitch the ball using your full arm circle. Your hips will turn, following your hand, with the hand finishing at your belly button.

Diamond Girl

THE SCREWBALL

The screwball is similar to the curve ball in that it will also break either into or out of the strike zone. The break is the opposite of the curve ball. The curve ball breaks away from a right-handed batter whereas the screwball will break *towards* a right-handed batter. Pitchers use this pitch to try to "jam" the right-handed batter, forcing the batter to hit the pitch off of the handle of the bat. Depending on the location of the release of the ball, the ball may either travel on a horizontal plane if you use a low follow-through, or rise and break towards the batter if your finish is high.

There are various grips for the screwball and personal preference dictates which grip to use. Most pitchers prefer either a two- or four-seam grip. Some pitchers will also curl their index finger but most pitchers leave the index finger lying flat along the seam.

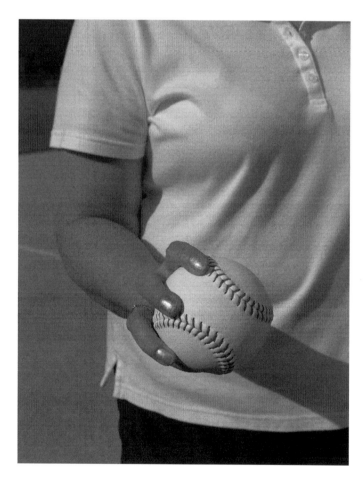

Fig. 13.13 The screwball grip.

The stride land is key to the proper rotation of the ball. The stride land for the curve ball was across the power line, whereas the stride land for the screwball must be sideways - on the *glove-hand side* of the power line. Your balance needs to be over the stride leg as your head slightly tilts towards the direction

Advanced Pitching: Adding Movement Pitches

of your pitch. The path of your pitching arm and release point will be close to the stride leg. You "stir the pot," as they say, since your pitching arm will follow close to your stride leg. Due to your sideways stride location, this will create a sideways release and an off-balance finish.

Fig. 13.14.a The correct stance to throw the screwball is shown.

Fig. 13.14.b Notice the step and the closeness of the pitching hand to the stride leg.

Practicing the screwball:

Drills from previous pitches can be easily used to work on the screwball. Learning the spin is quite easy if you focus on spinning the ball as quickly as possible. Larger softballs may help to see the correct movement while smaller softballs may help to develop the correct release.

1. Stand with your stride leg on the glove-hand side of the power line. Practice going through the path of your pitching arm, "stirring the pot," keeping your arm close to your stride leg. Move to the pitcher's mound and practice stepping sideways as you go through your arm circle.

Diamond Girl

2. Place a cone or a noodle about 10 feet in front of home plate. Try throwing the ball around the left side of the object. Then alternate throwing the curve ball (which will travel around the right side of the object) and the screwball (which travels around the left side of the object).

Master the four main pitches and the use of location before adding the curveball and screwball.

CHAPTER 14
The Pitcher/ Catcher Team

How important is the pitcher?
- The game of softball doesn't begin until the pitcher throws the first pitch.
- The pitcher dictates the rhythm of the game.

You began preparing for the game by practicing the drills in this book. Pitchers need to know their strengths and weaknesses and continually work to improve. However, it's important to remember that even though you are at the top of your game, you are only one person on the field. It takes a whole team to win or lose.

There are also tips and tricks you can use to give you and your team the edge in any game.

You and your catcher.

You and your catcher are the "battery" that makes the team run like a well-tuned engine. You and your catcher are basically another smaller team within the confines of a larger team. The two of you need to work together to figure out a way to keep the batter from getting on base.

Your catcher is closest to the batter and can pick up possible signs of weaknesses. For example, she can observe the batter's stance, the way she's swinging the bat in her warm-up, and the way she's gripping the bat.

You, from the pitcher's point of view, can also pick up possible weaknesses from your position on the pitcher's mound. Notice how far the batter's bat extends over home plate in her warm-up swings. Does she have an upward swing or a downward "chop" swing? Does she stand straight or bend over? Does she seem anxious to hit the ball?

Because of the catcher's position and her ability to closely assess the batter, the catcher calls the pitches. She will also take into consideration the game situation as well and which pitches are working. You, the pitcher, have the option to change the pitch the catcher has called. There may be something you picked up from studying the batter, or you received a tip from someone that the batter can't hit a certain pitch. You may have faced this batter in a previous game and know her weakness. Or, you may not have complete confidence in throwing the pitch the catcher calls and feel another pitch would also work. If you and your catcher are pretty much on the same wavelength, the next signal she indicates will be the pitch you thought about throwing.

Keep in mind that it may take time to figure out what the batter doesn't like. Both you and your catcher need to make mental notes of what works and what doesn't work for each batter. You will face these batters more than once during a game so it's best to have a plan. The best time to discuss how you want to handle the upcoming batters is between innings.

Before throwing even the first pitch, you need to find out the rules your league requires for taking signals from the catcher. For instance, do your hands need to be separated before stepping onto the pitcher's rubber? Does your league require you to take signals from the catcher while standing on the pitching rubber?

If your hands need to be at your side when stepping onto the pitching rubber bring your hands together chest level as soon as possible and tuck the ball in your glove in order to hide the ball from the batter. Remember that advanced batters will not look at your windup, but will study where you release the ball. The longer the batter can see where your release point is the greater the chance of you becoming a pitching machine.

If your league requires you to take signals from your catcher while standing on the pitcher's mound, your catcher *can* give you a signal as to *where* to stand on the pitcher's mound before you even approach the rubber. For instance, if you want to throw an inside pitch to a right-handed batter, stand on the left side of the pitching rubber in order to get a better angle towards the batter's hands, making her hit the pitch off the handle of the bat. In other words, to get a better angle on your pitch, move to either side of the pitching rubber.

Pitching from a Catcher's Perspective

Jaime Wohlbach began her catching career in 1997 while attending Kutztown University in Pennsylvania. Since then, she has had an extensive background in national and international competition. Jaime is a former professional player for the Philadelphia Force, California Sunbirds, and the Tampa Bay Firestix. Her international experiences include playing for teams from Italy, Greece, Czechoslovakia, and Holland. She also has an international coaching background for girls' teams from Australia, Switzerland, and Italy. Jaime is a former assistant coach for Lehigh University, the University of Pennsylvania, and Muhlenberg College.

The Pitcher/Catcher Team

She is the former head softball coach at Iona College, New York, and is currently the head softball coach at the University of Delaware.

Jaime most graciously accepted an invitation to answer a few questions on pitching from a catcher's perspective.

Q: Explain the importance of how a pitcher and catcher need to work together, beginning with preseason work through the game experience.

A: I always like to refer to the pitcher and catcher as a "battery." There is a positive and negative charge, and without one another, there is no power. Obviously, the goal of a pitcher and catcher is to keep that battery at full charge.

In preseason, the pitcher and catcher work on two forms of communication: verbal and body movement. Verbal communication refers to common phrases that will help refocus and encourage a pitcher during the game. Body movement on the part of the catcher helps give the pitcher a target for where the pitch should be thrown. It also affects the call the umpire will make on a pitch, and therefore it is extremely important for a catcher to know how to position her body for each pitch in a pitcher's repertoire. Furthermore, during preseason the catcher needs to learn the pitcher's "go-to" pitch. Learning which pitches a pitcher is most confident throwing enables a catcher to focus a pitcher during a tough game situation and get the needed out. Preseason work involves strength and stamina with both a pitcher and a catcher. As an example, if a pitcher throws a lot of rise ball pitches, her catcher will need to "pop-up" from her squat, which requires strength and stamina on the part of the catcher. At the same time, a pitcher works on her wrist snaps, leg drive, and other physically demanding aspects of her game.

It is just as important for a pitcher to focus on wrist snaps, spin, and movement during preseason as it is for a catcher to practice receiving a pitch, framing, and blocking. With both a pitcher and catcher the goal is to develop a strong skill set during the preseason so that game situations are a combination of muscle memory, confidence, and adrenaline rush from competition.

By the time the season begins, the goal is to have the pitcher and catcher in a groove. When I play, and I get in this groove, it's as if I can just feel what pitches the pitcher is expecting me to call. This is what preseason workouts are all about…developing this type of camaraderie and confidence between the pitcher and catcher.

Q: What is a typical pre-game warm-up for a pitcher and catcher?

A: First, a pitcher and catcher do team running and stretching with the team. Then we break off from the team and begin with wrist snaps. Each pitcher will differ with how quickly she warms up, but in about 10 wrist snaps, we move on to walk-throughs. (Note: walk-throughs are where the pitcher takes a few steps before throwing the ball, literally "walking through" her complete

Diamond Girl

pitching motion.) After walk-throughs a pitcher will work on each pitch, working a pitch until the pitcher is comfortable with that particular pitch. As a catcher, a lot of pitchers that I've caught end their warm-up with a "superstitious" pattern of pitches that they've developed through their career before going in the game. For example, a pitcher who throws one pitch to every corner of the "box" and ends the sequence with a change-up.

Q: Pitchers like having both location and movement of the ball in a game but that doesn't always happen. Which do you feel is more important – location of the pitch, or movement of the ball?

A: Both are equally important. Especially because in any given game, a pitcher might not have the movement she wants or be able to hit her spots with a specific pitch. So, if one aspect of the pitcher's game is not working (such as movement) then the other (location) needs to compensate.
    For a pitcher that has little movement but hits location, a catcher needs to work with the pitcher by zoning a pitch or, for example, climbing the ladder. This helps a pitcher with just location to be effective.

Q: Do you feel it is more advantageous for a coach to call the pitches, or the pitcher/catcher call their own game? Why?

A: As a catcher, I prefer to call my own game. From a catcher's perspective, we can see the pitch location and movement better than a coach who is viewing from the dugout. Also, working with an umpire and understanding their strike zone is part of a catcher's role – many times a catcher's body position and glove angle determines the call, and this can help a pitcher and catcher get into their groove on the field.
    However, I believe a catcher needs training in this area to understand the game situation, i. e. why a pitch is being called in certain situations. A catcher must always know the pitch count, how many outs, the score, the pitcher's "go to pitch," and more. If a catcher is inexperienced or depending on the coach's coaching style, the coach might prefer to call all pitches. There are many factors that play into a coach's decision such as if a coach did extensive scouting on a team, the coach will know which pitches to throw to each batter.

Q: What part does the catcher play in helping the pitcher make corrections to their mechanics on and off the field?

A: This ties into the important lessons and understanding a pitcher, catcher, and coach learn during preseason trainings. For example, during preseason a catcher may have learned that a pitcher needs a reminder to use her leg drive more when she gets tired. In a game situation, a catcher calls a timeout to give a quick reminder to 'use your leg drive'.

The Pitcher/Catcher Team

Q: You've caught for pitchers from your college days through your professional career. What is one of the toughest bad habits for a pitcher to break?

A: There are two bad habits that immediately come to mind. The first bad habit is a physical bad habit: when a pitcher jerks her shoulder for movement (especially with a drop ball), when the pitcher should be getting the movement from her wrist. This habit can potentially cause a pitcher to injure her shoulder.

The second bad habit involves mental game. As a specific example, a pitcher who is unable to stay poised on the mound when the umpire makes a bad call. A lack in mental game in this situation can cause a pitcher to lose her focus and miss her next pitch.

Q: Which pitcher did you enjoy catching the most? Why?

A: Amy Kyler, a pitcher on the NPF California Sunbirds team, was one of my favorite pitchers to catch. Not only did she throw hard (about 69 MPH) but she also had a lot of movement. She had a tough mental game and was determined to beat her opponent. She was very poised on the mound, making her a true leader on the field. Furthermore, her speed made it difficult for hitters to make contact.

As a catcher these aspects of Amy Kyler's game encouraged me to be at the top of my game both physically and mentally. Due to Amy's velocity and movement on her pitches, I needed to be quick and sharp behind the plate to receive pitches.

Q: What advice can you give to beginner pitchers as well as the more advanced pitchers of today?

A: For a beginner pitcher it is important to trust your catcher, be confident in your catcher and to take it all as a learning experience. The pitcher needs to learn to ask questions such as: Did I hit my spot? Did the pitch move? Did the pitch change speed?

For an advanced pitcher, it is imperative to develop strong communication with your catcher. It is important for a catcher to know a pitcher's strength and weakness, because on the field a catcher provides support, focus, and added confidence to a pitcher's performance. Also, remembering that the goal is to develop to keep that "battery" fully charged.

CHAPTER 15
Managing the Game

Mental preparation for the game.

It is said that playing sports is 90% mental and 10% physical. Mental preparation for a softball pitcher begins before you even set foot onto the pitcher's mound. You prepare physically by practicing the mechanics needed to throw different pitches, working on spins, correct body positioning, and location, as well as building stamina and endurance. Mentally you prepare by reviewing the coach's game plan and talking with your catcher, strategizing on how you want to handle the game. Maybe you played against this opponent in a previous meeting and know that the batters like to hit fast balls. Maybe you've seen this opponent play in another game and you know that the first two batters are extremely quick runners and like to slap-bunt.

Mental preparation doesn't stop once the game begins. During the game, a pitcher and catcher need to constantly review which pitch the batter hit in their previous at bat. Together, you and your catcher may be able to figure out the batter's weakness and make necessary adjustments with pitch selection.

The pitcher needs to remain calm and confident. Forget the last bad pitch you threw, the walk or hit you just gave up, the error your teammate just committed (remember you are just as capable of making an error as well), how you just struck out, or that it's beginning to rain. Forget the past and focus on what *you* can do better in the next inning, or the next game. Every game is a learning experience. Treasure the lessons! They will make you a better pitcher.

Diamond Girl

Mental preparation for throwing the pitch.

There are three things to remember before actually throwing the pitch. First, review the mechanics of the pitch in your mind. Review what each part of your body should be doing as well as the location of your release point. Second, visualize the path the ball needs to travel from your release point to your catcher's glove. Visualize the power line from your starting position on the pitching rubber to your target. Third, clear your mind and throw the ball.

Your first step is with your stride leg and should always be down your power line *towards your catcher's glove*. Your pivot foot will follow with your hips facing your catcher's glove.

Do NOT rush between pitches. Make each pitch count by following the above mentioned three steps to throwing the pitch.

The pitch count.

The count on the batter will dictate whether the batter or the pitcher has the advantage. The count will also dictate which pitch you need to throw. (Note: the first number indicated in the pitch count chart on page 95 means how many balls are on the batter; the second number indicates strikes.)

The best pitched game is one where you *appear* to throw strikes. Try to keep ahead in the count so the batter has to keep guessing what your next pitch may be. You don't necessarily have to strike out the batters but you want them to hit *your* pitch – one that will produce a ground ball or a fly ball to one of your fielders.

"Cheat Sheet" for Pitchers

There are certain locations in the strike zone in which the batter feels comfortable swinging at the ball. For the most part you want to try to stay out of those zones. Batters will show you which pitches they do or do not like without realizing it. Batters will also try to force you to throw into their preferred hitting zones. At that point you may need to throw a pitch just outside of their preferred zone in order to get them to chase the ball.

The "cheat sheet" on page 96 mentions a few situations for determining which pitch may work in getting the batter out. Don't forget that a high fastball can be substituted for the rise ball.

Managing the Game

PITCH COUNT	PITCHER'S RESPONSE
No count	As a pitcher, you hope to get ahead in the count by throwing a strike, usually a fast ball, hitting one of the corners. Most batters will not swing at the first pitch.
0-1	Throw your best pitch outside of the strike zone. Hopefully the batter will chase a pitch to get to 0-2.
0-2	You are in control since you now have pitches to waste to get the batter to swing at a pitch outside the strike zone. Try pitches the batter has to chase such as the riser or drop pitch.
1-1	Throw a pitch close to the strike zone, working the corners again to get the batter to chase it. You have leeway to give up more balls before walking the batter.
2-1	The batter has the upper hand since you don't want to go 3-1. Throw one of your best pitches close to the strike zone.
2-2	You have control because the batter must protect the plate and not let another strike go past. A pitch such as a change-up or rise ball outside the strike zone would be a good pitch to throw.
1-2	You have the advantage, giving you a number of options as to what pitch to throw. Work the corners with a pitch that appears to be a strike such as a rise ball, curve, or drop pitch. If the batter is behind on her swing with your fastball, a fastball would work well. The change-up may also work if your fastball is working well. Sit the batter down as quickly as possible.
1-0	Advantage goes to the batter. Throw your best pitch to a corner, or some type of good movement pitch. Just don't throw down the middle of the plate.
2-0	Advantage again goes to the batter. You have no choice but to throw a strike since you don't want to fall deep into the count. A hard fastball where the umpire has been calling strikes is needed. If the umpire has been calling low strikes, throw it there.
3-0	Ugh! This is not a good situation for the pitcher! You have no choice but to throw a hard fastball down the middle and hope the batter will take the pitch or miss it if they swing.
3-1	No room for you to breathe. You're still in a tricky situation. You need to throw a strike or something that looks like a strike.
3-2	The fate of the batter comes down to this pitch. You need to throw a great pitch at a good location in order to make the batter swing or go down looking.

Cheat Sheet

BATTER'S STANCE	PITCHER'S REACTION
1) Batter stands close to home plate	Throw the ball inside. The batter will have a hard time hitting pitches close to her body since the sweet spot of her bat extends over the outside corner. She will need quick wrists to bring the bat around fast enough to hit the inside pitch.
2) Batter stands away from home plate	Throw the ball to the outside corner. The batter will have to reach with her bat in order to hit the ball solidly.
3) Batter stands deep in the batter's box	Throw a drop pitch. Pitches break at the front of home plate. By the time she's realized a drop pitch was thrown, she has already swung over or hit only the top of the ball.
4) Batter stands in the front of the box	Throw a riser or high fast ball through and out of the strike zone. Because of the sharp upward angle of the pitch, the batter will either miss the ball or hit the bottom of it.
5) Batter stands bent at the waist	The batter is hunched over and can easily see a low pitched ball. Throw a riser or high fast ball.
6) Batter stands completely straight	The batter likes high pitches but won't be able to reach a low pitch. Throw a low fast ball across the knees or a drop pitch.
7) Batter digs in hard with her feet and takes numerous quick practice swings	The batter wants to swing for the fences and is anxious to do so. She wants to hit the fast ball. Throw a change-up or some type of off-speed pitch to catch her off balance.
8) Running slap hitters (these are hitters that begin in the left batter's box, trying to slap the ball between the third baseman and the pitcher for a hit; their main objective is to get a jump on the ball as they begin their sprint to first base)	These batters are moving through the batter's box and are looking for a pitch down the middle of the plate. You need to throw a pitch they have to reach for in order to keep these speedy runners off the bases. A high inside rise ball or a low outside pitch is suggested.
9) Bunting situation	The objective of this batter is to move the runners into scoring position. A pitch she is forced to reach for is needed such as a high pitch, or a low outside pitch.

Practice your defense!

Pitching is your primary responsibility, but not your only responsibility. Once you pitch the ball, you now become an infielder. Your job is to field softballs hit up the middle of the infield, field bunts, back up third base and home plate on throws from the outfield, and cover home plate on a passed ball or wild pitch. You even become part of run-downs, or "pickles," between bases. You need to work on your reflexes in order to become a better fielder. It is important to have someone hit softballs to you – grounders, line drives, bunts, and pop-ups – so that you learn to react to any situation. The distance from you and the batter is 35 to 43 feet, depending on the level of play. You don't have time to think about fielding the softball. You only have time to react.

Before each pitch you need to review the game situation in your mind. For instance, you need to know how many outs there are. Are the base runners fast or slow? If the ball comes to you where do you make the play? Will you need to back up a play if the ball is hit to the outfield? You need to know your responsibility as a fielder in all situations.

You must also be vocal, assisting with communication on the infield. For instance, there is a pop-up between the first and second basemen and nobody has called to catch it. You need to make a snap judgment as to who is in a better position to catch the ball and call out her name loud and clear. Call her name several times if needed.

Don't be afraid to remind your first and third basemen to be ready for a bunt if the situation calls for it. Don't be afraid to give your shortstop a "heads up" in case the base runner may consider stealing second base. This not only helps your teammates, but it also keeps your mind alert and in the game.

A pitcher's job is complex. The only way to be on top of your game is to *practice, practice, practice*!

CHAPTER 16
Going Back to Basics

There will be times when you don't seem to have much wrist snap, the drop pitch doesn't drop, the rise ball seems to hang directly in the hitter's zone, or you simply can't hit the location you want. Every pitcher goes through a difficult phase at some point in time. Don't get discouraged! Pitching problems mean you need to go back to the basic mechanics in order to make the necessary corrections to get back on track.

Here is a list of some of the most common pitching problems along with solutions for correcting them. Please consult the section of the book indicated and practice those drills. You may have to refer to more than one section since multiple problems are linked.

BASIC PROBLEMS	DRILLS TO CORRECT PROBLEM
1) Pitching hand finishes flat. Fingers curl into the palm of your hand.	Wrist snap drills – page 10
2) Body leans forward while releasing the ball. Hand finishes flat.	Balance drills – page 35 Wrist snap drills – page 10

3) Pitcher uses a bent elbow through the arm circle.
    Arm is away from body and out of the power line.
    Speed of arm circle is inconsistent.
	Arm circle drills – page 24

Diamond Girl

BASIC PROBLEMS	DRILLS TO CORRECT PROBLEM
4) The pitcher's body stays square to her catcher (doesn't open her hips down the power line). Pitching arm hits hip on downswing. Pitcher develops sore pitching shoulder.	Hip rotation drills – page 29
5) Pitcher's arm is tense and stops at her hip. She uses her elbow to throw the ball. Follow-through is tense.	Arm circle drills – page 24 Relaxation drills – page 65 Wrist snap drills – page 10
6) The stride foot is off the power line. Body leans forward upon release.	Stride drills – page 42 Hip rotation drills – page 29 Balance drills – page 35

For problems with the moving pitches, please see the following pages reading the introductory pages of each pitch as well as the specific drills.

Fast ball – page 64
Change-up – page 66
Drop pitch – page 71
Rise Ball – page 75
Curve Ball – page 81
Screw Ball – page 84

Pitching begins and ends with proper mechanics. Your pitching career began by practicing the basic mechanics mentioned at the beginning of this book. As you progressed, you began adding movement to the ball practicing the proper mechanics of the grips and spins. Pitching is not easy and it takes a lot of dedication. You need to decide for yourself whether you want to be a "thrower" or a "pitcher." You will only be as good as you want to be.

BIBLIOGRAPHY

Stevens, Mona R., *Fastpitch Pitching Drill Book*, South Haven, Mississippi: S&W Printing, 1993.

Workman, Paul, "*The Psychology of the Count*", Fast Pitch World Magazine, June 1994.

Kendrick, Scott. "Jennie Finch – Profile of USA Softball Pitcher Jennie Finch." 2010.
    <http://baseball.about.com/od/olympicsoftball/p/jenniefinch.htm>

Xinhua News Agency. "Jennie Finch, ace pitcher with three Olympic golds." 1 August 2008.
    <http://www.china.org.cn/olympic/2008-08/01/content_16114136.htm>

The New York Times. "Athlete Bio: Jennie Finch." 3 August 2008
    <http://www.nytimes.com/2008/08/03/sports/olympics/biofinch.html>

The Official Website of Jennie Finch. "Jennie's Biography." 2003-2006.
    <http://www.jenniefinch.net/bio.htm>

"Cat Osterman." 2008.
    <http://www.thesoftballchannel.com/starspotlight/catosterman.html>

Email communication with Jaime Wolbach, former professional catcher and currently Head Softball Coach at University of Delaware, Newark, DE, December 17, 2009.

Made in the USA
San Bernardino, CA
17 February 2014